INNOVATIVE TECHNOLOGIES

HYDROGEN AND FUEL CELLS

ABDO
Publishing Company

INNOVATIVE TECHNOLOGIES

HYDROGEN AND FUEL CELLS

BY REBECCA HIRSCH

CONTENT CONSULTANT

Cliff Ricketts, PhD
Professor of Agricultural Education
School of Agribusiness and Agriscience
Middle Tennessee State University

CREDITS

Published by ABDO Publishing Company, PO Box 398166, Minneapolis, MN 55439. Copyright © 2013 by Abdo Consulting Group, Inc. International copyrights reserved in all countries. No part of this book may be reproduced in any form without written permission from the publisher. The Essential Library™ is a trademark and logo of ABDO Publishing Company.

Printed in the United States of America,
North Mankato, Minnesota

112012
012013

 THIS BOOK CONTAINS AT LEAST 10% RECYCLED MATERIALS.

Editor: Rebecca Felix
Series Designer: Craig Hinton

Photo Credits: PRNewsFoto/American Honda/AP Images, cover; iStockphoto/Thinkstock, 6, 43; Shutterstock Images, 11, 46; Ben Russell/iStockphoto, 14; Bettmann/Corbis/AP Images, 16; Archive Holdings Inc./Getty Images, 20; AFP/Getty Images, 24; Russell Clark/Alamy, 27; AP Images, 28; Thomas Kienzle/AP Images, 31; Charles Shapiro/Shutterstock Images, 33 (top); Terry Renna/AP Images, 33 (center); LovelaceMedia/Shutterstock Images, 33 (bottom); Panoramic Images/Getty Images, 34; Charles D. Winters/Getty Images, 40; Red Line Editorial, 51, 71; MCT/McClatchy-Tribune/Getty Images, 54; Josh Reynolds/AP Images, 56; AP Photo/Lockheed Martin Missiles & Space/AP Images, 58; Anthony Upton/Press Association/AP Images, 63; Craig Ruttle/AP Images, 64; Zoonar/Thinkstock, 66; Encyclopedia Britannica/UIG/Getty Images, 69; Kyodo/AP Images, 75, 85; Sjoerd van der Wal/iStockphoto, 76; UIG/Getty Images, 79; Katsumi Kasahara/AP Images, 80; Richard Drew/AP Images, 89; Damian Dovarganes/AP Images, 90; Michael Sohn/AP Images, 95; GIPhotoStock/Getty Images, 96; Johannes Eiselle/AFP/Getty Images, 99; Thomas Samson/AFP/Getty Images, 101

Library of Congress Cataloging-in-Publication Data
Hirsch, Rebecca E.
  Hydrogen and fuel cells / Rebecca Hirsch.
     p. cm. -- (Innovative technologies)
  Audience: 11-18.
  Includes bibliographical references.
  ISBN 978-1-61783-464-6
  1. Hydrogen as fuel--Juvenile literature. 2. Fuel cells--Juvenile literature. I. Title.
  TP359.H8H57 2013
  665.8'1--dc23
                          2012024010

>> TABLE OF CONTENTS

CHAPTER 1

WHY HYDROGEN?

Today's world is hungry for energy. People depend on energy to power their cars, heat and cool their homes, run factories, charge cell phones, and do countless other things. All over the world, demand for energy continues growing, fueled by a growing population. In addition, the two most populous countries, China and India, are industrializing. That means people are moving from farms and rural areas into cities to work in newly built factories. More industry means more demand for energy. With all of these changes, energy use worldwide is expected to skyrocket.

In the United States, demand for energy is high and rising as well. Although the US population makes up only 5 percent of the world's population, US citizens consume almost 25 percent of the world's energy.[1] Demand for energy in the United States has nearly tripled since 1950 and is likely to increase further in the coming years.[2]

« As nations become industrialized and populations grow, more buildings are constructed and more cars are on the road.

Fossil fuels—oil, natural gas, and coal—account for most of the world's energy use. These fuels are burned to power vehicles and heat homes and businesses. They are used to make electricity to run devices like computers, televisions, and air conditioners.

But fossil fuels are generally considered to be nonrenewable energy sources. They are made from the remains of plants and animals that lived hundreds of millions of years ago, and their supplies are limited. New supplies of fossil fuels would take hundred of millions of years to be created. As world energy demand rises, reserves of fossil fuels are running out.

Even if fossil fuels could last forever, their use still creates problems. Sourcing energy from fossil fuels makes the United States dependent on foreign sources. The United States cannot produce enough oil to meet its needs, and it imports more than half of its oil from other parts of the

"Energy is the single most important problem facing humanity today. We must find an alternative to oil. We need to somehow provide clean, abundant, low-cost energy to the 6 billion people that live on the planet today, and the 10-plus billion that are expected by the middle of this century."[3]
—Richard E. Smalley, winner of the 1996 Nobel Prize in Chemistry, speaking before Congress in 2002

world.[4] This dependence on foreign sources makes the country vulnerable. In the 1970s, war and other problems in the Middle East led to reduced supplies and soaring gasoline prices in the United States.

THE GREENHOUSE EFFECT AND POLLUTION

Another issue with fossil fuels is their effect on the atmosphere. Fossil fuels contain hydrocarbons, which are molecules made of carbon and hydrogen. When the fuels are burned they give off carbon dioxide, an invisible gas that then becomes part of the air. This creates smog and acid rain. Nearly half of all people in the United States live in areas where air pollution is high enough to harm the environment or endanger human health.[5]

These emissions also affect global warming, an increased warming of the earth. Earth's atmosphere is made of a mixture of gases. Some gases, such as carbon dioxide, absorb heat. These are called greenhouse gases. By absorbing heat, these gases warm the air, producing what is called the greenhouse effect. This is a natural part of life on Earth. If it weren't for

CLIMATE CHANGE AND THE ENVIRONMENT

During the twentieth century, Earth's average temperature increased approximately 1 degree Fahrenheit (0.6°C). While this may seem like a small or insignificant amount, small changes in temperature mean big changes for the environment. Climate change has already had a noticeable impact. Glaciers are retreating, sea ice is shrinking, sea levels are rising, ice on rivers and lakes is breaking up earlier, and heat waves are growing more intense. The Intergovernmental Panel on Climate Change (IPCC), the leading scientific organization for the assessment of climate change, predicts a temperature rise of 2.5 to 10 degrees Fahrenheit (1.4 to 5.6°C) over the next century, which would create even more environmental changes.[6]

greenhouse gases, all of the radiated heat would escape back into space, and Earth would be much chillier than it is.

But today, more and more carbon dioxide is being released into the air through the burning of fossil fuels. Earth's average temperature is increasing, and a large body of scientific evidence shows that a major cause of the warming is the release of carbon dioxide from fossil fuels. In other words, burning fossil fuels is accelerating the natural greenhouse effect.

The prospect of continued climate change is of great concern to many scientists, environmentalists, and government officials. Most people agree that something should be done about our fossil fuel use soon. One of the major possible solutions is to shift away from fossil fuels and instead use fuels that do not add greenhouse gases to the environment. The ideal alternative fuel would be powerful, abundant, inexpensive, and free of carbon dioxide emissions. Many people think that fuel is hydrogen.

WHAT IS HYDROGEN?

Hydrogen is a simple element. All elements are made of atoms. Atoms consist of different combinations of protons, electrons, and neutrons. Hydrogen atoms are made up of just one proton that makes its nucleus, or center, and one electron that surrounds it like a cloud. It is the lightest element in the periodic table, existing almost always as a gas that is colorless,

A hydrogen atom: one electron surrounds a proton in the nucleus.

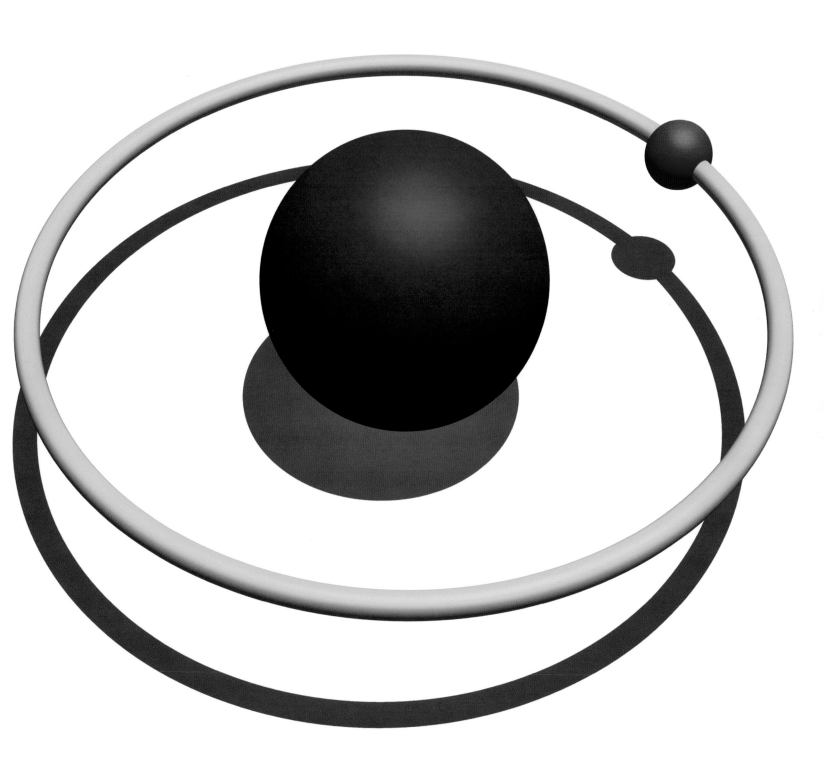

odorless, and nonpoisonous. Hydrogen gas can also be turned into liquid hydrogen at a very low temperature: minus 423 degrees Fahrenheit (–253°C). Supplies of hydrogen are potentially limitless. Hydrogen is very abundant in the universe, making up 75 percent of all mass and 90 percent of all atoms.[7] The sun is made primarily of hydrogen. So are the planets Jupiter, Saturn, Uranus, and Neptune.

SIMPLE ATOM: HYDROGEN

All matter in the universe is made of atoms, which are tiny particles too small to see. Atoms are made of even smaller particles called protons, neutrons, and electrons. Protons, which have a positive charge, and neutrons, which have no charge, are in an atom's center, or nucleus. Electrons, which have a negative charge, travel around the nucleus. Different elements contain different numbers of protons, neutrons, and electrons. Hydrogen is the simplest element. It is made of one proton, one electron, and no neutrons.

But because it reacts easily with other elements, hydrogen is rarely found by itself on Earth. It naturally combines with other elements to form compounds. For example, hydrogen combined with oxygen creates water. Combined with carbon, hydrogen is present in the organic compounds that make up all living things and are abundant in fossil fuels.

The hydrogen in fossil fuels is what delivers power. When these hydrocarbon-rich fuels are burned, hydrogen and carbon are both released from the hydrocarbon molecules. The hydrogen combines with oxygen in the air to form water, and energy is released. The carbon is released as carbon dioxide emissions.

Pure hydrogen gas, or H_2, made of two hydrogen atoms joined together, can also be burned. But unlike fossil fuels, burning pure hydrogen gives off no carbon dioxide; the only byproducts are heat and water, because the hydrogen combines with oxygen.

Unlike coal and oil, hydrogen is not an energy source on its own. An energy source is something that contains stored energy, which can be removed through a chemical reaction such as burning and used as fuel. A fuel stores extracted energy so that it can be transported to another location and used at another time. For example, oil is an energy source, and the gasoline extracted from it is a fuel. In the same way, water is an energy source, and the pure hydrogen extracted from it is a fuel.

To produce pure hydrogen gas for use as fuel, the hydrogen must be freed from its bonds with other elements. Separating the elements to produce hydrogen requires the use of another form of energy. This is one disadvantage to using hydrogen as a fuel. Because other sources are needed to produce hydrogen, the process is not always free of greenhouse gas emissions. Although burning hydrogen fuel does not pollute the air, the sources used to produce the fuel itself might. Producing hydrogen is therefore one of the biggest challenges in using this

fuel. In addition, hydrogen is difficult to transport and store, which drives up the cost of using hydrogen.

Some scientists, politicians, and visionaries dream of a hydrogen economy, which is a vision of a world in which hydrogen is used to power nearly all things, including homes, businesses, and cars. Widespread use of hydrogen will only happen if there are inexpensive ways of transporting, storing, and using it and clean ways of producing it. Scientists and engineers around the world are working hard to overcome the challenges presented by the production and use of hydrogen. They are using innovative methods to produce hydrogen from alternative energy sources. They are engineering high-tech ways to store and transport hydrogen and designing innovative fuel cells, devices that produce power using hydrogen, for everyday use. Understanding hydrogen's successful and failed uses in the past is a first step in developing new ways to produce and use hydrogen as a fuel.

 Hydrogen is most often used as a gas, which can be a challenge to transport and store.

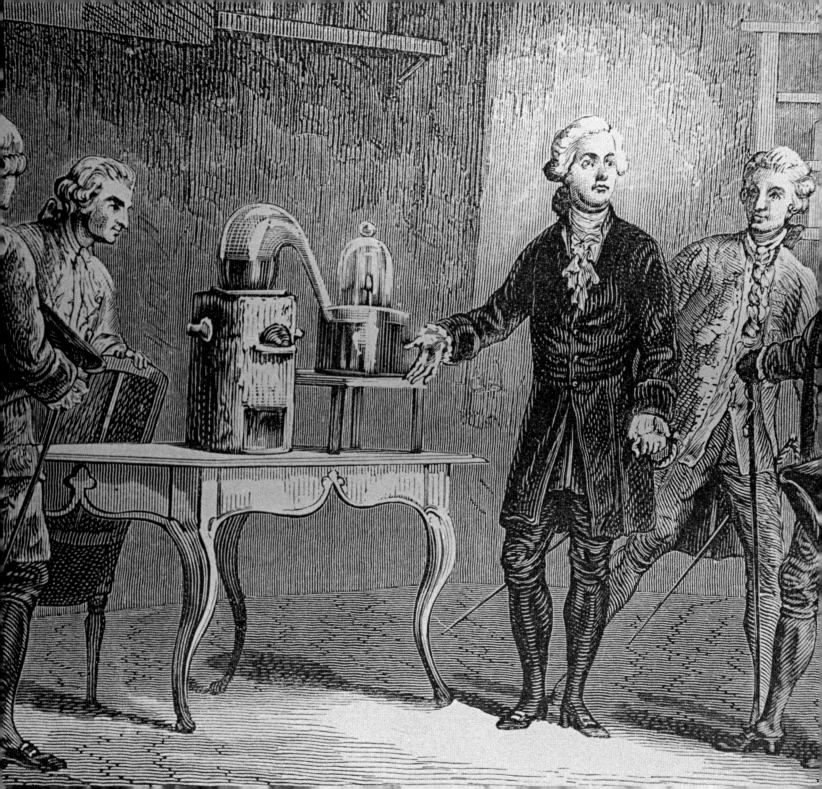

CHAPTER 2

THE HISTORY OF HYDROGEN

The first person known to produce hydrogen was English scientist Robert Boyle. In 1671, he made a gas as he experimented with mixing metals with acids. Unknown to Boyle, it was hydrogen gas, produced by certain strong acids when they react with any metal. Boyle may have been the first person to produce hydrogen, but the man most often credited for discovering it is English scientist Henry Cavendish. In 1766, he collected hydrogen, which he described as inflammable air, by combining zinc or iron with acids and then accurately describing its properties.

French chemist Antoine Lavoisier later discovered that this inflammable gas was a component of water. Since ancient times, people had believed water to be a basic element along with fire, air, and earth. In 1783, Lavoisier turned that idea on its head when he proved that water could be made by burning hydrogen in air. Lavoisier realized

« **Antoine Lavoisier presenting a water experiment in the eighteenth century** this meant water was made of hydrogen and oxygen. He also proved the reverse was true: water could be broken down into hydrogen and oxygen. His experiments proved water was not a basic element but instead a combination of two gases. Lavoisier also gave hydrogen its name. The word hydrogen comes from the Greek *hydro* and *gene*, which put together mean "maker of water."

CHARLES'S LAW

Jacques Charles was well known during his lifetime for his work with balloons, but today he is best known for a scientific law that bears his name. As Charles experimented with hydrogen balloons, he noticed something about gases. As a gas warms, it expands. As a gas cools, it shrinks. In other words, Charles realized that hot gas takes up more space than cold gas. Today this observation goes by the name Charles's Law: at a fixed pressure, the volume of a certain amount of gas is proportional to its temperature.

FIRST HYDROGEN TRANSPORT

The first person to use hydrogen for transport was another French scientist, Jacques Charles. In 1783, the same year Lavoisier made his breakthroughs, Charles launched the world's first hydrogen balloon. To produce enough hydrogen, he poured hydrochloric acid into a barrel full of iron filings, creating a chemical reaction that produced hydrogen gas. Charles collected the hydrogen gas given off in a cloth balloon, which caused the balloon to rise. On August 27, 1783, Charles launched the unmanned balloon from the Champ de Mars, a large military parade ground in Paris. Many people gathered to watch and cheer. Soon after the balloon's launch, a violent storm began, and the balloon shot straight up beyond the clouds and was lost from view. Less than an hour later, the balloon landed in a village 15 miles (24 km) away, where frightened peasants—unused to seeing large objects float down from the sky—attacked and destroyed it with pitchforks.

The first manned flight in a hydrogen balloon came just a few months later, when Charles and his instrument maker flew for two hours and traveled nearly 30 miles (48 km) before descending safely north of Paris.

THE *HINDENBURG*

In the 1930s, a tragedy caused people to question hydrogen's safety. At the time, hydrogen-powered airships had caught on in Germany as a means of travel. These structures were held in the air by a lighter-than-air gas, such as hydrogen or helium, and looked similar to today's flying blimps. The airships used a concept similar to Charles's early hot-air balloons, using hydrogen gas for lift, except the airships could be steered. Before World War II (1939–1945) broke out in 1939, Germany's hydrogen-filled airships were used to ferry passengers between Europe and the United States. They were considered a luxury way to travel.

THE *HINDENBURG*

The *Hindenburg* was the largest airship ever to fly, as tall as a 13-story building and more than two football fields in length. It was designed to be inflated with helium. Hydrogen was substituted when the United States, the world's largest producer of helium, refused to sell helium to Germany after World War I (1914–1918). On the *Hindenburg*'s last voyage it was filled with 7 million cubic feet of pure hydrogen gas—enough to lift the ship itself plus over 200,000 pounds of passengers, crew, and cargo. When the ship caught fire only 62 of the 97 people on board survived. While there is a generally accepted theory, no one knows exactly why the explosion started. Although many cameras captured the explosion, none of them captured the start of the fire.

The largest of the German airships was called the *Hindenburg*. It made ten round-trip voyages across the Atlantic in 1936. Then on May 6, 1937, the *Hindenburg* suddenly caught fire over Lakehurst, New Jersey. In only 32 seconds the airship burned to rubble. Thirty-six people died. The disaster was captured on film, and people would later watch the footage over and over. The horrific disaster became linked in many people's minds with hydrogen and likely stalled widespread acceptance of hydrogen as a fuel.

To this day, although there are many theories, no one knows exactly why the *Hindenburg* caught fire. In 1997, Addison Bain, a retired National Aeronautics and Space Administration (NASA) engineer, and William D. Van Vorst, professor emeritus of chemical engineering at University of California, Los Angeles, challenged the commonly believed idea that hydrogen, which is highly flammable, caused the fire. Bain believed that although hydrogen did burn in

The Hindenburg airship explosion on May 6, 1937

the disaster, it was not the cause of the fire. He explained that the *Hindenburg*'s airframe was covered in a cotton skin, which was then coated with an extremely flammable substance—the same substance used as a burning-rate catalyst in rocket boosters.[1] According to a UCLA news release on the two men's theory, there was an additional provoking agent. "The manner in which the skin was attached to the airframe allowed a large electrostatic charge to build up on its surface. When it finally discharged, it did so with disastrous results," stated the release.[2] Bain and Van Vorst believe these factors were the cause of the disaster.

HYDROGEN IN THE TWENTIETH CENTURY

The twentieth century brought many advances in the use of hydrogen as a fuel. Although hydrogen had been used as a fuel as early as the eighteenth century, German engineer Rudolf Erren advanced its practical use and its popularity. In the late 1920s, he began experimenting with ways to convert the internal combustion engines (ICEs) of cars, buses, and trucks to run on hydrogen gas or mixtures of hydrogen with other fuels. Erren converted thousands of vehicles that could run on either hydrogen gas or hydrocarbon fuels with the flip of a switch. But the work ended with the onset of World War II.

The US Air Force began experimenting with hydrogen fuel for spy aircraft in the 1950s. The air force found that hydrogen-powered aircraft were small, light, and quiet. But in the late 1950s, the nation's attention shifted to space rockets, and the program ended.

In the 1960s, hydrogen found a home in the space program as rocket fuel. Hydrogen's lightness made it an obvious choice for launching rockets, where the main objective is overcoming gravity. But NASA also had to overcome enormous technical challenges to use hydrogen as rocket fuel. One is that liquid hydrogen must be kept very cold—if it becomes warmer than minus 423 degrees Fahrenheit (–253 °C), it turns to gas and escapes. Any source of heat—exhaust from a rocket engine, friction with the air, heat from the sun—presents this danger. Because of this, hydrogen fuel tanks must be extremely well insulated. The storage tank also must be designed to withstand the extreme cold, which can make metals brittle.

Additionally, when liquid hydrogen does absorb heat, it expands. In order to prevent the tank from exploding due to accidental heating,

LAUNCHING ROCKETS

Each launch of a space shuttle consumes about 370,000 gallons (1.4 million liters) of liquid hydrogen weighing more than 200,000 pounds (90,000 kg). The combustion temperature reaches 5,800 degrees Fahrenheit (3,200°C).[3]

the gas that is created must be vented. NASA worked to devise ways to overcome all of these challenges, and since the 1960s, hydrogen rocket fuel has been used to launch space shuttles, probes, and satellites. Also in the 1960s, NASA engineers were looking for a way to provide electricity for manned space missions. A device called a fuel cell turned out to be ideal for the job.

FIRST FUEL CELLS

Early uses of hydrogen fuel were met with limited success due to the challenge of storing and transporting the light, gaseous substance that can escape from an ordinary container. But in the 1830s a scientist invented a device that would deliver an easier way to harness the power of hydrogen: the fuel cell.

A fuel cell is a device that turns chemical energy into electric energy, somewhat like a battery. Unlike a regular battery, a fuel cell never dies. It has holes in the top and bottom for adding the fuel. There are many types of fuel cells today, many of which use hydrogen as fuel.

The development of the first hydrogen fuel cell began when William Grove, a Welsh lawyer and scientist, figured out how to create electricity by combining hydrogen with oxygen in the 1830s. It was well known in Grove's time that water could be split by electricity, using a technique called electrolysis. Electrolysis was simple: run an electrical current through water,

« **The Apollo shuttle was launched with hydrogen in 1969. From that decade forward, NASA has used hydrogen to launch its spacecraft.**

and hydrogen and oxygen gases bubbled out of the water. Grove realized the reverse reaction would also work: hydrogen and oxygen could be combined to make electricity.

To test his idea, Grove took two platinum strips and sealed the end of one in a tube of hydrogen and the end of the other in a tube of oxygen. Then he dipped the free end of each strip in a bottle of dilute sulfuric acid. At once a small amount of electricity began to flow between the strips.

Encouraged, Grove linked 50 of these devices in series to increase the voltage, calling his invention a gas voltaic battery. However, the device did not produce the amount of power Grove anticipated, and he eventually abandoned his work.

Intrigued with Grove's invention, scientists and inventors tried to turn it into a practical device. Despite several attempts, a design for workable fuel cells did not emerge until the 1880s. Ludwig Mond and Charles Langer improved Grove's design, and they coined the term "fuel cell" in 1889. Despite the name change, fuel cells are similar to batteries because they create electricity from a chemical reaction. Fuel cells use the energy from a reaction between hydrogen and oxygen. Not all of the early fuel cell designs used pure hydrogen as a fuel. Coal and coal gas, a hydrogen-rich mixture of gases obtained from coal, were also used.

A statue of William Grove stands in a park in Surrey, England, as a tribute to his pioneering fuel cell technology.

Research on fuel cells continued through the late nineteenth century, although the devices failed to find practical use as they could not compete with other means of making electricity. Hydroelectric and steam power were inexpensive and could be used to make huge amounts of electricity. Batteries were simple and inexpensive. Fuel cells, by contrast, were complicated devices, and the precious metals used to make them were expensive.

During the first half of the twentieth century, researchers continued to experiment with different ways to make fuel cells. In the 1930s, Francis Bacon, a British engineer, began tinkering with fuel cell design. As Grove had before him, Bacon experimented with hydrogen-oxygen fuel

Francis Bacon and his
fuel cell design in 1959

cells, units that produced power through the reaction of hydrogen with oxygen. Bacon replaced
the expensive platinum with inexpensive nickel gauze and substituted potassium hydroxide for
the sulfuric acid, which tended to eat away at the platinum electrodes. Through the changes
he made, Bacon invented the first alkaline fuel cell. Over the course of many years, Bacon
developed the alkaline cell to the point that he could carry out large-scale demonstrations of its
usefulness, beginning in 1959. The most notable of these was a tractor that was powered by a
stack of 1,008 cells and could pull a weight of approximately 3,000 pounds (1,400 kg).[4]

In the 1960s, scientists worked to develop other types of fuel cells. These included the proton exchange membrane (PEM) fuel cell and the phosphoric acid fuel cell (PAFC), both of which used hydrogen as fuel. Various types of hydrogen-powered fuel cells would eventually be used to provide power for power plants, buildings, and vehicles. Alkaline cells and PEM cells were also used by NASA to power the electronics on board spacecraft. They also produced drinking water for the crew as a byproduct of their chemical reaction.

Since the 1960s, fuel cells have been used again and again in space travel. PEM fuel cells were used on some of the flights of the Gemini program, which ran from 1962 to 1966 with missions beginning in 1964, but these early designs had many technical difficulties. Engineers switched to alkaline fuel cells to power the electronics on the rockets in the Apollo program. The Apollo space program ran from 1963 to 1972, and missions ran from 1968 to the end of the program. Its missions successfully landed the first people on the moon. Alkaline cells were also used to power the space shuttle missions that launched from 1981 to 2011.

At approximately the same time NASA began using fuel cells on spacecraft, carmakers began experimenting with using fuel cells to power vehicles. Before this time, researchers had used fuel cells to power a tractor, a golf cart, a submersible, and a forklift. In 1966, General Motors created the first car powered by a hydrogen fuel cell, the Electrovan. The car could reach 70 miles per hour (113 km/h) and could travel a distance of 150 miles (241 km) before refueling.[5] The Electrovan, however, was never practical enough to be offered to consumers. For one thing, the fuel cell required so much expensive platinum that the cost was enough to buy a fleet of vans.[6] For another, the size and weight of the fuel cell and its supporting parts were prohibitive. The outfit contained some 550 feet (168 m) of plastic tubing as well as cryogenic tanks to store liquid hydrogen and oxygen. The potassium hydroxide electrolyte alone weighed 550 pounds (249 kg).[7] But an even bigger problem may have been that there was no supporting infrastructure at the time—there were no places where drivers could recharge the fuel cell with liquid hydrogen. Other carmakers also developed their own experimental fuel cell vehicles, but none of these early cars were ever sold to customers. Meanwhile, many carmakers were also experimenting—and finding much greater success—with other alternative vehicle models, including electric and hybrid vehicles. Research into fuel cell vehicles began to wane.

Then, in the 1980s, Canadian geophysicist Geoffrey Ballard formed Ballard Power Systems. He focused his attention on developing a fuel cell that could power vehicles at a similar level of performance to an ICE. The company made technical breakthroughs in fuel cell design, and in the 1990s they put municipal buses powered by fuel cells on the roads in Vancouver, British Columbia, and in Chicago, Illinois. These moves launched the modern fuel cell era. Ten years

German car company Daimler Benz signed an agreement with Ballard Power Systems in 1997 to develop fuel cell buses such as this one that were similar to the Ballard design.

later, in 2003, hydrogen-powered cars became a reality when US car manufacturer Honda released the first fuel cell car for commercial use.

Fuel cell research continued throughout the first decade of the twenty-first century, and many advances were made. As development of hydrogen fuel and hydrogen-powered fuel cells continued, many people dreamed of a hydrogen economy—the total system needed to create a world fueled by hydrogen. But although many innovations have successfully used hydrogen as a fuel, great challenges—particularly how to produce, store, and transport it—remain. To understand the obstacles for future use, traditional methods for producing hydrogen, and their promises and pitfalls, must first be examined.

HYDROGEN PAST AND PRESENT

1671–Boyle produces hydrogen by exposing metals to acids.

1766–Cavendish identifies hydrogen as a distinct element.

1780s–Lavoisier splits water into oxygen and hydrogen and recombines them again to make water. He gives hydrogen its name in 1788.

1783–Charles travels in the first manned hydrogen balloon.

1839–Grove develops the first hydrogen fuel cell, using hydrogen to make electricity.

1937–The *Hindenburg*, a hydrogen-filled German airship, bursts into flames while landing in Lakehurst, New Jersey.

1959–Bacon demonstrates an alkaline fuel cell.

1960s–Hydrogen fuel cells provide onboard power for the Gemini and Apollo spacecraft and all subsequent space missions.

1963–The first hydrogen-powered rocket, the Centaur, is launched.

1966–General Motors develops the first fuel cell car.

1993–Ballard Power Systems releases the first fuel cell bus in Vancouver.

1997–Bain and Van Vorst challenge the idea that hydrogen caused the *Hindenburg* accident.

2003–Honda releases the first hydrogen fuel cell car approved for commercial use.

INNOVATION

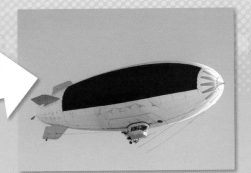

While airship use as a luxury means of travel dwindled after the *Hindenburg* accident, airship technology forged on. Today, airships are still in use, now often called blimps. One company has developed an all-weather airship that can land virtually anywhere at land or sea.

INNOVATION

Hydrogen has remained an important part of spacecraft launches. Today, hydrogen is utilized in rockets, which attach to spacecraft for launch and then detach, returning to Earth. NASA has developed many innovations in the storage, compression, and use of hydrogen, including using hydrogen to provide onboard electric power and oxygen for spacecraft crewmembers.

INNOVATION

Since its inception, fuel cell technology has improved and many innovations have emerged. Fuel cell vehicle research continues to advance, and the shells of many of these vehicles look as cutting edge as their technology under the hood.

CHAPTER 3

HYDROGEN PRODUCTION AND USES

Today, more than 11 million short tons (10 million metric tons) of hydrogen are produced in the United States each year.[1] Most hydrogen is used in industrial processes such as refining oil, making ammonia for fertilizer, synthesizing methanol, and hydrogenating vegetable oils. Very little is used as fuel. The main use of hydrogen fuel is to propel rockets into space.[2] A tiny amount of hydrogen fuel is used to provide power for homes, businesses, and vehicles.

Pure hydrogen must be made from raw materials that contain hydrogen, such as hydrocarbons or water. Separating the hydrogen from another element requires a form of energy. Sources of energy used to make hydrogen today include fossil fuels as well as alternative energy sources such as wind and solar power. These energy

A hydrogen plant in Salt Lake City, Utah, provides hydrogen and steam to refineries in the surrounding area.

sources provide the power needed to separate elements. Each way of producing hydrogen has advantages and disadvantages.

NATURAL GAS REFORMING

The bulk of hydrogen produced in the United States today—approximately 95 percent—is made from reformed natural gas.[3] Natural gas is a fossil fuel consisting mainly of the chemical compound methane. Methane is made up of one carbon atom and four hydrogen atoms, the compound CH_4. To convert methane to hydrogen, natural gas is treated with steam at high pressure. This breaks the chemical bonds between carbon and hydrogen, releasing hydrogen gas, which can be collected to use as fuel. Carbon is also released as carbon dioxide.

HYDROGENATION

One non-energy use for hydrogen is hydrogenation. When hydrogen atoms are added to fatty acids, it changes the fat from a liquid into a solid. This is how margarine and shortening are made from vegetable oil. Treating fats this way gives them a longer shelf life.

Natural gas reforming has rapidly advancing technology and an extensive natural gas pipeline system that is already in place. A disadvantage is the process produces carbon dioxide emissions. Because of these emissions, hydrogen made by this method cannot reasonably be considered an environmentally safe fuel. What's more, the process of separating hydrogen also requires high temperatures, which take large amounts of energy to create. If that energy also comes from fossil fuels, then the carbon dioxide emissions are even greater.

Hydrogen can also be made from other fossil fuels, such as gasoline or coal, but this process also produces carbon dioxide. Carbon emissions are a major disadvantage to using fossil fuels to produce hydrogen. Still, some experts believe making hydrogen from fossil fuels could be a step in the right direction. To make the process safer for the environment, the carbon dioxide could be piped underground where it cannot pollute the atmosphere. Carbon dioxide capture would make the process of making hydrogen this way much safer for the environment, but it would also drive up the cost of hydrogen even further.

BIOMASS GASIFICATION

Biomass energy includes crops grown for energy, such as corn or switchgrass. It can also include waste such as farm residues, wood scraps, or food scraps. Biomass is often considered renewable, because, as the US Energy Information Administration (EIA) states, "We can always grow more trees and crops, and waste will always exist."[4] It is important, however, that these resources are sourced in a way that does not negatively affect the environment.

Steam and high heat can be used to break down the materials in biomass and produce hydrogen in a process called biomass gasification. Although carbon dioxide is also released from

USING SOLAR POWER IN BIOMASS GASIFICATION

Producing hydrogen by biomass gasification uses high-temperature reactors that typically draw energy from coal-fired power plants. If hydrogen produced from biomass is to be environmentally safe, the energy to power the reactors must come from a renewable energy source. Teams of researchers have launched a project using solar energy to power the reactors. The solar energy is collected and then concentrated. "It's basically similar to using a magnifying glass to concentrate sunlight to a point, although we use mirrors instead of lenses," Carl Bingham of the National Renewable Energy Laboratory in Golden, Colorado, told *Biomass Magazine*. The process can generate temperatures greater than 3,632 degrees Fahrenheit (2,000°C).[7]

biomass, the biomass itself removed carbon from the air during its growing season, so the net carbon dioxide added to the atmosphere is reduced to nearly zero.[5] There are drawbacks to biomass, such as the amount of land that must be set aside for fuel. The cost of growing, harvesting, and transporting biomass is high too, making this method more expensive than natural gas reforming. The high temperatures and pressures needed make it possible only on a large scale, and currently the amount of hydrogen squeezed out of biomass is low because the amount of hydrogen in biomass is low: just 6 percent, compared with 25 percent for natural gas.[6] To be competitive, the process needs to be made more efficient, and the cost must be reduced. The process must also become more flexible to work with a range of waste products and their variations. Additionally, biomass gasification requires large amounts of electricity, which can be counterproductive or create greenhouse gas emissions if not derived from a clean energy source such as solar or wind.

ELECTROLYSIS

Water, the combination of hydrogen and oxygen, is another source of hydrogen production. Making hydrogen from water is done by electrolysis. The process of electrolysis is carried out in an apparatus called an electrolytic cell, or often an electrolyzer. Electrolysis starts with water that has had a small amount of electrolyte added. The electrolyte can be a small amount of dissolved sodium or sodium hydroxide. Pure water cannot be used because it does not conduct electricity well. Two electrodes are dipped in the water, and a catalyst is added to aid the water-splitting reaction. The reaction begins when an electric current is run between the two electrodes. The electricity flows from the anode, which is the positive electrode in this type of reaction, to the cathode, which is the negative electrode. As electricity flows, it causes a chemical reaction, and the water splits into hydrogen and oxygen. Oxygen gas collects at the anode and hydrogen gas gathers at the cathode. The hydrogen that bubbles up then gets collected and used as fuel.

Electrolysis as a way to produce hydrogen has distinct advantages and disadvantages. Its source—water—is abundant, safe for the environment, and cheap. The process of electrolysis,

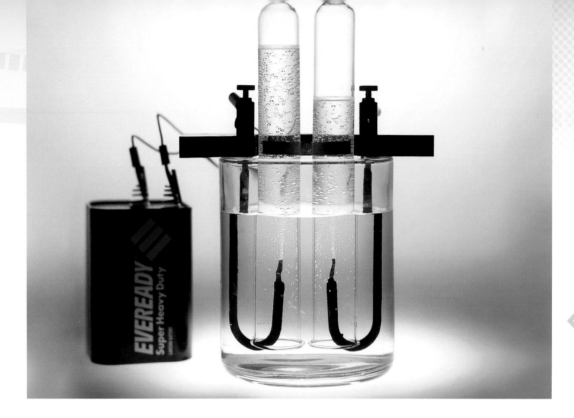

«

Electrolysis of water: oxygen and hydrogen are separated using electricity.

however, is expensive because it requires a catalyst to aid the water-splitting reaction. Currently the best material for catalyzing the reaction is platinum, which costs $1,500 an ounce.[8]

The isolated process of electrolysis does not produce harmful greenhouse gases, which is an advantage. Electrolysis does require electricity, however, and most of the electricity in the United States today is made by burning fossil fuels, which creates carbon dioxide emissions.

To realize hydrogen's promise as a nonpolluting fuel, it must be produced in ways that do not emit carbon dioxide and do not further increase the world's dependency on fossil fuels. For electrolysis this means obtaining electricity from a clean source. Only then can the hydrogen produced be considered green. Fortunately, clean options exist for creating the electricity needed for electrolysis.

ELECTRICITY FOR ELECTROLYSIS FROM NUCLEAR ENERGY

Nuclear power is one energy form that can supply the electricity for electrolysis. As of 2012, it provided 20 percent of the electricity produced in the United States.[9] Nuclear power plants make electricity using the energy of fission, the splitting apart of the atoms of certain elements into smaller parts. When these atoms split during fission, energy is given off. That energy is used to boil water and create steam, which turns turbines to generate electricity.

Nuclear energy is a massive source of power. Uranium is the substance that undergoes nuclear fission in a nuclear plant. Uranium is so powerful that an amount roughly the size of the tip of an adult's little finger packs more energy than 1,700 pounds (770 kg) of coal.[10]

Nuclear energy also does not produce carbon dioxide. What it emits instead, however, is a cause of concern to many. To create nuclear energy, radioactive materials are used. These materials emit radiation during fission. If a large amount of radiation is released outside a power plant, it can be dangerous to people and the environment, causing health problems and even death from overexposure. The nuclear fission process also creates radioactive waste materials, some of which remain radioactive for thousands of years. Concerns over the threat of radioactive materials leaking into the environment and how to safely store the radioactive waste that these power plants produce are major issues surrounding electricity production from nuclear energy. Public confidence in nuclear power lessened after nuclear power plant accidents that leaked radioactivity occurred at Three Mile Island in the United States in 1979, Chernobyl in the Ukraine in 1986, and Fukushima in Japan after a large earthquake in 2011. Although nuclear energy has appeal as an energy source that would alleviate dependence on fossil fuels and emit no carbon emissions, it remains controversial. Therefore, sourcing the electricity needed for electrolysis from nuclear power remains problematic.

ELECTRICITY FOR ELECTROLYSIS FROM RENEWABLE ENERGIES

Another way to produce clean electricity for electrolysis is through renewable energy sources. If solar and wind energy are used to produce the electricity to make hydrogen, the hydrogen becomes a completely carbon-free fuel, meaning no carbon dioxide was produced to make it. Many people believe linking hydrogen production with renewable energies such as solar and wind power may be the ideal partnership.

Solar and wind energy have great potential. It is estimated electricity from US wind power could produce enough hydrogen to exceed current US gasoline consumption.

Solar power is the conversion of sunlight into electricity using solar cells, devices that capture the energy from sunlight and use it to make electricity. Wind power is converted from wind energy by turbines. Wind turbines capture the energy from wind using blades that spin a shaft that makes electricity. The electricity made from wind or solar could then be used for electrolysis to make hydrogen.

One disadvantage to solar and wind power is that these sources are not constant or reliable. The sun does not always shine, and the wind does not always blow. What could help solve this problem, however, is the hydrogen produced from electricity provided by these energies. When electricity from solar or wind power is available, hydrogen can be produced by electrolysis. The hydrogen can then be stored and used to produce electricity with a fuel cell during times when sunlight or wind is not available. Hydrogen could be a convenient energy carrier that could be moved from place to place. Batteries are another option for storing electricity, although large quantities of electricity cannot be stored using existing battery technology. Hydrogen can be used to store huge amounts of electricity, although the storage and transport of hydrogen comes with its own challenges.

However, no energy source is perfect, and these renewable sources come with their own costs and benefits. It is a big challenge to make hydrogen in ways that are earth friendly and inexpensive. Solar energy is abundant, but harvesting it is currently expensive. Most solar cells require silicon, which is expensive to produce. Wind energy is cheap, and in recent years the makers of wind turbines have made huge advances in reducing the cost further. But wind power is not widely available because not all places are windy and not all sites are suitable for large turbines. Large-scale solar and wind energy both also require large amounts of land. While carbon dioxide emissions are avoided, the challenge of producing hydrogen from these sources will be to do so cheaply and on a large scale.

WORLDWIDE HYDROGEN PRODUCTION

This pie chart depicts the sources of energy used to make hydrogen as of 2005.[11]

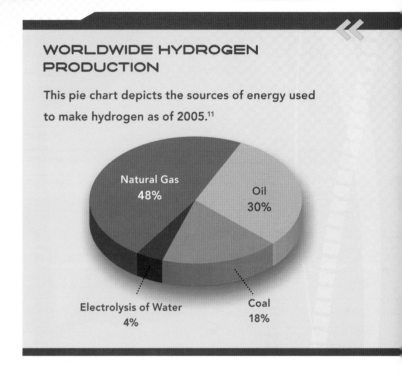

Natural Gas 48%

Oil 30%

Coal 18%

Electrolysis of Water 4%

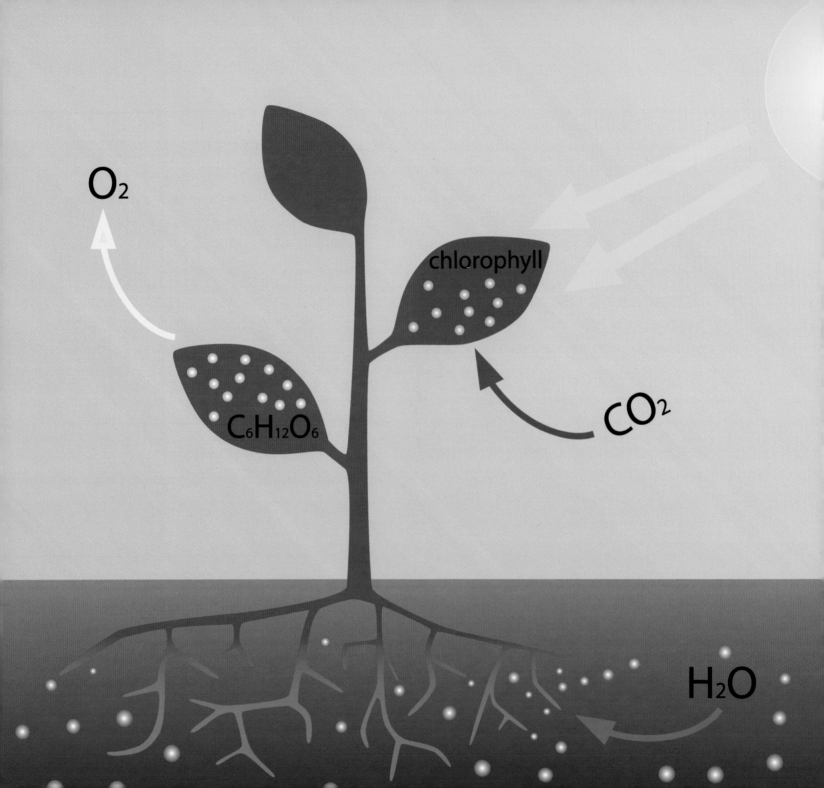

CHAPTER 4

NEW HORIZONS IN HYDROGEN PRODUCTION

Researchers are exploring innovative new ways to make hydrogen from clean sources. They are also finding ways to solve pitfalls in current production processes from clean sources. One innovative approach uses devices that convert sunlight directly into hydrogen fuel. Another uses the power of microorganisms to produce hydrogen. These technologies, and many others, are still being researched and have not yet found practical use outside the lab, but that could soon change. Someday, these methods could be used to produce hydrogen fuel to help power the planet.

ARTIFICIAL PHOTOSYNTHESIS

The sun is an abundant source of energy. "More energy from the sun hits the earth in one hour than all the energy consumed on our planet in an entire year," said Nathan S. Lewis, a chemist from the California Institute of Technology.[1] In addition to creating

The process of plant photosynthesis

the electricity needed for electrolysis, research into using the sun's massive energy to directly produce hydrogen is underway, using plants' food processing as a model.

Green plants tap into the sun's abundant energy through photosynthesis, the process that provides the energy for nearly all life on Earth. Using air and water as raw materials and energy from sunlight, plants produce sugars. These sugars are the plants' food, a fuel that helps them to grow. A plant that makes its own food is called a producer. Animals that eat these plants, as well as the animals that eat those animals, are consumers. They, too, depend on photosynthesis to provide the energy they need to survive. Photosynthesis gives off oxygen, which animals and people need to survive. The photosynthesis process does not produce any greenhouse gases.

HYDROGEN IN THE SUN

The sun provides the energy that powers life on Earth. That energy comes from a nuclear reaction involving hydrogen: the fusion of two hydrogen atoms into helium. The sun's core is filled with hydrogen. The core is very hot—more than 27 million degrees Fahrenheit (15 million°C)— and very tightly packed. The intense pressure forces hydrogen atoms to come together and combine to form helium. This reaction creates most of the sun's energy. That energy reaches Earth as radiant energy, giving us light and heat, and provides energy for plants to grow, which is passed along to nearly all life on Earth.

Photosynthesis begins as plants soak in the energy from sunlight. Plant cells have a compound called chlorophyll that traps the sun's energy. Along with sunlight, the plant takes in water from its surroundings and carbon dioxide from the air. During photosynthesis, the water molecules are split into pure hydrogen and oxygen. The plant releases the pure oxygen into the air. The hydrogen fuses with carbon dioxide to create glucose, a type of sugar, which the plant uses as food. Scientists are drawing inspiration from this process as they search for new ways to use the sun's energy in hydrogen production.

Currently, using solar energy to make hydrogen typically requires two steps. First, solar energy is used to make electricity. Then the electricity is run through an electrolyzer placed in water. The electrolyzer splits the water into oxygen and hydrogen. But now researchers are building devices that, like plants' leaves, can do this all in one step. The devices are called photoelectrochemical (PEC) cells, and they can be thought of as artificial leaves. They convert solar energy to chemical fuel (hydrogen) in a way that is similar to how plants do. Unlike plant

STORING SOLAR

Solar power is a viable alternative energy, both on its own and as energy for producing hydrogen, but efficient storage has been a consistent problem. According to Nathan S. Lewis, a professor of chemistry at the California Institute of Technology, "We have to find a way to really cheaply capture, convert, and store sunlight. Because without storage . . . we don't have an energy system. That's the challenge we face from science and technology."[2] However, one program at Middle Tennessee University has found a way to benefit from solar power long after it is captured. Through the Tennessee Valley Authority's Generation Partners Green Powerswitch program, which incentivizes and supports wind and solar power installations, the university produces solar power to add to the state's electrical grid. The university is paid for the solar energy it produces in energy credits, and it is able to later purchase electricity with those credits to use for electrolysis.

leaves, which convert and store the sun's energy as sugars, PEC cells convert and store the sun's energy as hydrogen. PEC cells skip the second step of plant photosynthesis, which is the combining of hydrogen and carbon dioxide to make sugar. Instead, the end product of a PEC cell is pure hydrogen and pure oxygen.

PEC cells have two elements: a solar collector that converts the sun's energy into electricity, and an electrolyzer that splits water into oxygen and hydrogen. Catalysts, such as chemicals or metals, are also needed to aid the reaction. When the PEC cell is placed in a clear jar of water and put in the sun, streams of hydrogen and oxygen bubble to the surface.

Researchers have made exciting progress in developing these devices. John Turner at the National Renewable Energy Laboratory in Golden, Colorado, built one that produced so much hydrogen, it was 12 times as efficient at carrying out photosynthesis as a plant leaf.[3]

But these early PEC devices were not affordable enough for everyday use. The collectors that capture the sun's energy require silicon and the electrolyzers use platinum as a catalyst. Both elements are expensive. Although Turner's device was super-efficient, it cost as much as $10,000 per square centimeter.[4]

The process of artificial
photosynthesis in a PEC cell

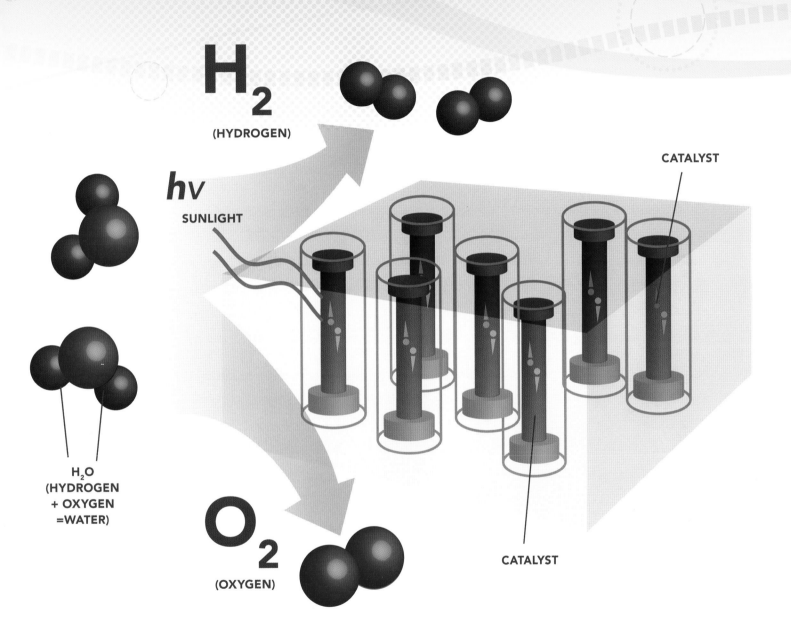

H~2~ (HYDROGEN)

$h\nu$
SUNLIGHT

H~2~O
(HYDROGEN
+ OXYGEN
=WATER)

O~2~
(OXYGEN)

CATALYST

CATALYST

Durability has been another challenge. Splitting water is highly corrosive, meaning it eats away at the electrodes in the electrolyzer. Turner's PEC cell wore out in less than a day.

Researchers have been working hard to overcome the challenges of these devices. In 2011, Daniel Nocera of the Massachusetts Institute of Technology unveiled the first practical PEC cell, a unit the size of a playing card. The device made by Nocera's team is made of materials that are cheaper and last longer. For catalysts it uses the elements cobalt and nickel, both of which are abundant and inexpensive. The materials do not wear out quickly, and the device can operate continuously for at least 45 hours.[5] The device is also remarkably efficient: ten times more efficient than a leaf at performing photosynthesis.[6] Nocera thinks his team can improve that efficiency even further. As of 2012, Nocera's device has not yet been commercialized.

PEC innovations for producing hydrogen from solar energy include inexpensive solar sheets that could be installed on a rooftop, allowing homes to create hydrogen from sunlight. The sheets would collect solar energy and use it to make electricity. Extra energy would be used to split water into hydrogen and oxygen, and the hydrogen and oxygen could be stored in separate tanks. Later, when the sun is not shining, a home fuel cell would recombine the stored hydrogen and oxygen and make electricity. The entire system enables the homeowner to overcome one of the big difficulties of solar—getting 24 hours of energy from what is only a daytime energy source.

An idea to produce hydrogen from PEC cells on a larger scale is to build solar power plants near coastal cities and produce hydrogen from seawater. The hydrogen produced could be fed through a fuel cell power plant. The fuel cell would make not only electricity, but, because a byproduct of a hydrogen-powered fuel cell is water, the plant could also make water for drinking.

"To make hydrogen efficiently on a large scale . . . we will ultimately need solar. Nuclear, biomass, wind, hydroelectric—they don't have enough capacity to make a dent in global energy needs. With solar, there's an unlimited supply."[7]**—Tom Mallouk, Penn State University**

MICROORGANISMS

Another innovation in hydrogen production is using certain species of microorganisms to split water and produce hydrogen. One way to do this is with microorganisms that are photosynthetic, meaning they can carry out photosynthesis. Similar to green plants, photosynthetic microorganisms live off the sun, capturing energy from sunlight and using it to split water. These microorganisms make hydrogen during the reaction. Researchers are

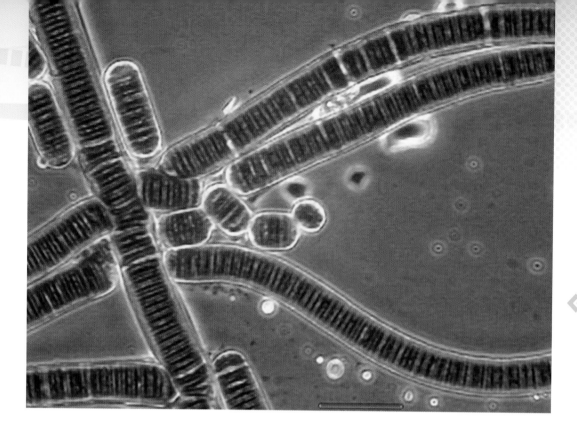

Microorganisms such as cyanobacteria, seen only under a microscope, naturally produce hydrogen during photosynthesis.

developing a system that can control and cycle these microorganisms' cells between the photosynthetic growing stage and the hydrogen production stage.

Researchers are studying how to grow microorganisms in bioreactors. The microorganisms could produce hydrogen at a low cost. The approach is in the very early stages of development. Currently, the water-splitting reaction from this approach is much too slow for commercial hydrogen production. Researchers are looking at ways to speed up the process, and they envision that someday the method could be used to produce hydrogen sustainably. But as of 2012, this process was not yet being used commercially.

Another way to put microorganisms to work is through fermentation. Certain microorganisms can break down organic matter, releasing hydrogen. Researchers at Penn State University have successfully produced hydrogen by allowing hydrogen-producing microorganisms to ferment wastewater from food processing plants. The microorganisms feed on organic matter in the wastewater and produce a gas rich in hydrogen. The team used ordinary soil as a source of microorganisms, heat-treated to kill all bacteria except the hydrogen-producing ones. The heat used to treat the soil is a very small amount relative to the energy output from the process. Wood chips, farm waste, and other biofuels can all be treated using microorganisms as well, turning the energy they contain into usable hydrogen fuel. Although the technique is not yet available for commercial hydrogen production, scientists are working to scale up and demonstrate the process for commercial use.

MICROORGANISMS

Hydrogen-producing algae and bacteria occur naturally in the environment. These microbes can be found in lakes, rivers, oceans, and even in melting snow. They are also widespread in soil.

POWERING FUTURE HYDROGEN PRODUCTION

With so many new options on the horizon for producing hydrogen without carbon dioxide emissions, in addition to the well-tested methods using cleanly sourced electricity, how will hydrogen be made in the future? Some experts think all ways of producing hydrogen will be viable options. "Not all hydrogen will be produced in one way," said Bruce Logan, a scientist at Penn State University. "It will depend on where you live—how much sun, wind, and biomass are around."[8]

Massachusetts Institute of Technology scientists present their research in hydrogen production from algae.

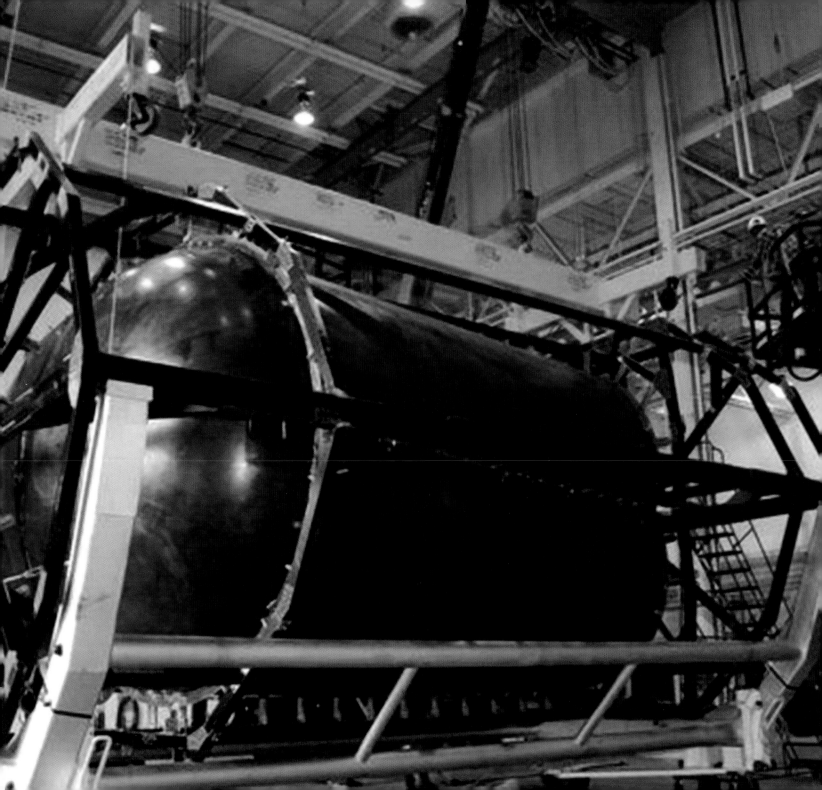

CHAPTER 5

HYDROGEN STORAGE AND TRANSPORT

O nce hydrogen is made, storage and transport are big challenges. It is not easy to store hydrogen. It is very light and takes up a large amount of space as a liquid or a gas. For certain applications, hydrogen's need for space is not a problem. Large tanks holding hydrogen are fine for stationary uses, such as in homes or businesses. Taking up a lot of space is also not much of a problem in space travel, where hydrogen has been used for decades. As writer Scott L. Montgomery put it, "The large tanks needed are not a drawback when your vehicle is the size of a skyscraper."[1]

But storage does become an issue when it comes to other types of transportation. A standard gasoline fuel tank holds approximately 15 gallons of fuel. A tank holding the same amount of energy from hydrogen fuel would need to contain 60 gallons.[2]

A prototype of a liquid hydrogen tank for an unmanned spacecraft. While liquid hydrogen takes up less volume than gas, storage tanks still need to be large.

One way around the volume requirement is to compress the hydrogen. Today, most hydrogen-powered vehicles use high-pressure tanks. Researchers have designed tanks that can safely hold hydrogen gas at high pressures. These tanks are still big and bulky compared to gasoline tanks, however.

Another option is liquefying the hydrogen. However, the temperature at which hydrogen becomes a liquid is so low that it is near absolute zero, which is the temperature at which all atomic motion stops. Creating conditions that cold takes an enormous amount of energy—up to 40 percent of the energy contained in the hydrogen itself.[3]

One of the most promising areas of research for hydrogen storage is using solid storage materials. Certain materials, such as metals, can form chemical bonds with hydrogen. Researchers are designing solid materials that can store hydrogen. Some solid storage materials are spongelike, with lots of nooks and crannies. Some are fluffy, similar to cotton candy. All of these materials might one day serve as ways to cram a large amount of hydrogen into a small space. Presently, the US Department of Transportation has not given general approval of solid hydrogen storage, also called metal hydride tanks, but has issued some individual permits for it.

DISTRIBUTING HYDROGEN

Another challenge in widespread use of hydrogen is distribution. Today, most hydrogen is made close to where it is used. This is because there is not yet an efficient way to move large amounts of hydrogen across long distances. Before hydrogen can be widely used as a fuel, better transportation methods must be developed.

Today there are two distinct ways to distribute hydrogen. One way is to make great quantities of it at large, central plants and then deliver it to where it is needed. Pipelines then carry the hydrogen over short distances or tanker trucks ship it over longer distances.

Some researchers have proposed using existing natural gas pipelines to transport hydrogen. But others believe this will not work. Hydrogen reacts with the metals in pipelines, making the pipes brittle. Many experts say these existing pipelines are much more effective at transporting natural gas than hydrogen.

STORING HYDROGEN IN ROCKS

Researchers are working on using rocks called zeolites to store hydrogen in fuel tanks. Zeolites have a honeycomb structure that allows them to act like sponges. They are used in water and air filters. They are also the odor-absorbing crystals in kitty litter. A fuel tank lined with zeolites might be able to trap and store hydrogen gas. Researchers are experimenting with growing zeolites in space, hoping to make zeolites that can hold large amounts of hydrogen.

The other option for distributing hydrogen is to make small amounts of hydrogen close to where it is used. This is called distributed generation. Instead of making hydrogen in a central location and then shipping it, hydrogen is made onsite where it is needed. Electrolyzers would be onsite, giving businesses or homes the ability to make the hydrogen they need. The sun, wind, or other renewable energies could power the electrolyzers.

British company ITM Power has made advances in creating small- and medium-sized electrolyzer units that are affordable. These units are about the size of an air-conditioner window unit. The company focused on using less-expensive materials in its electrolyzers, which brought down the cost of these units. It is working on a larger electrolyzer that could be used at fueling stations to make hydrogen for car and truck refueling.

HYDROGEN'S SAFETY

Many consumers will have to be convinced that hydrogen is safe in order for widespread use of hydrogen to take off. Although hydrogen actually has an excellent safety record, notable accidents, including the *Hindenburg* disaster, have given it a bad reputation among much of the public.

Hydrogen is both flammable and leak-prone, something that is true of gasoline as well. Static electricity or the operation of electronic devices can spark a fire. Despite this, hydrogen

The ITM Power CEO holds up the fuel nozzle of a larger model of the company's home electrolyzer units.

Hydrogen is successfully transported each day around the world, and tanks of hydrogen gas have proven to be safe even in the event of a leak.

has proven itself to be a safe fuel. Tanker trucks carry 70 million gallons (264 million L) of liquid hydrogen each year without major incident.[4] The Bellona Foundation, an environmental organization based in Norway, found that "hydrogen is no more or less dangerous than any other energy carrier" and that in certain areas it may actually be safer than other fuels, such as gasoline.[5]

To test hydrogen's safety, researchers at the University of Miami studied fuel leaks from cars powered by hydrogen and cars powered by gasoline. The results showed that hydrogen cars were less likely to catch on fire than those powered by gasoline.[6] Hydrogen's lightness makes it safe in the event of a fuel leak. When it leaks it does not pool or splatter, like gasoline does.

The escaping hydrogen gas quickly rises and expands, dispersing into a dilute concentration that is not dangerous. Unlike gasoline, hydrogen is nonpoisonous. A hydrogen leak will not cause pollution of air or water.

Research on safety and practical transportation of hydrogen continues. Meanwhile, the fuel cell is also undergoing innovations. Many believe advances in fuel cell technology may one day lead to widespread use of hydrogen as a fuel.

TESTING HYDROGEN'S SAFETY

To test the danger of fuel leaks in hydrogen cars, Dr. Michael Swain at the University of Miami set fire to two cars. One car was carrying gasoline and the other hydrogen. Before setting the cars on fire, Swain created fuel leaks that would be similar to what might occur in an accident. For the gasoline car, he poked a 1/16 inch (0.2 cm) diameter hole in the fuel line.[7] Simulating a leak in the hydrogen car was much more difficult. Hydrogen vehicles are designed with a number of safety features, such as leak-detecting sensors and shut-off valves. Nonetheless, Swain was able to create a leak at a pressure release valve. Then he set the cars on fire. What happened? The gasoline car was completely engulfed in an intense fire. The flame on the hydrogen car shot straight up and burned in the air, but the car was undamaged.

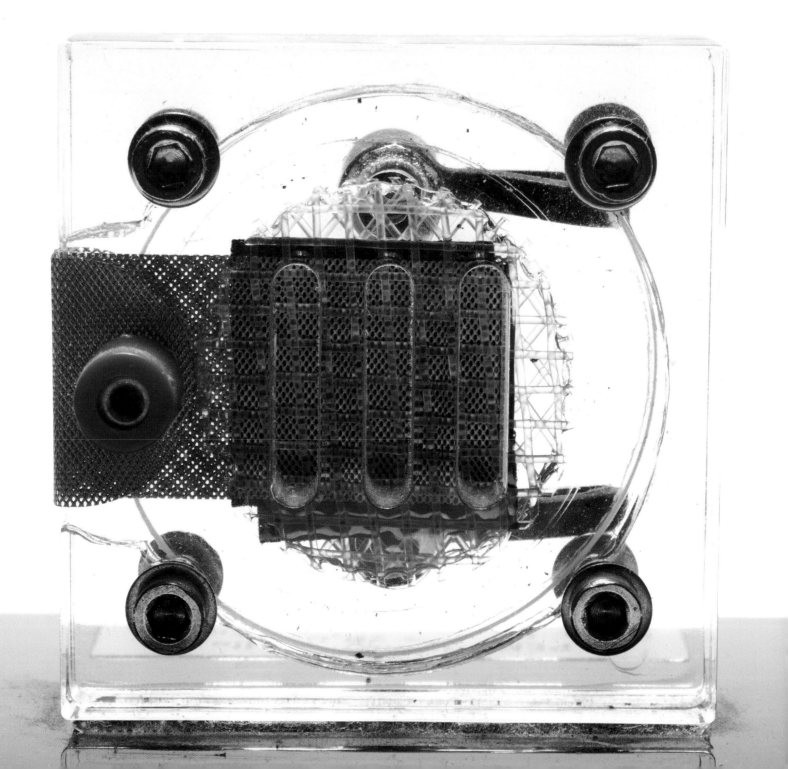

CHAPTER 6

FUEL CELLS

Fuel cells are similar to batteries because they use a chemical reaction to make electricity. Yet batteries and fuel cells work in different ways. Disposable batteries contain chemicals that react to produce electricity. When the chemicals run out, the battery is dead. Rechargeable batteries also use stored chemicals to produce electricity. They can be recharged by running electricity through the batteries. Fuel cells are different. They do not contain stored chemicals but require a constant flow of fuel.

"It works like a battery with holes in the top and bottom," says Matthew Mench, assistant professor of mechanical engineering at Penn State. "You flow fuel and air through it and it produces a steady current. Keep the flow going and it's always charged."[1] Unlike batteries, fuel cells never need to be recharged. As long as fuel is flowing, they can produce electricity.

« **A single fuel cell encased in plastic**

There are several types of fuel cells. All can use pure hydrogen as fuel, but some can operate on fuel mixtures that contain hydrogen. For instance, molten carbonate fuel cells can extract hydrogen from a variety of fuels. Solid oxide fuel cells can operate on fuel gases that contain hydrogen. Of the available types of fuel cells, proton exchange membrane (PEM) fuel cells, phosphoric acid fuel cells (PAFCs), and alkaline fuel cells (AFCs) are among the most common. They work by combining hydrogen and oxygen to produce electricity, giving off water and heat as byproducts.

PROTON EXCHANGE MEMBRANE FUEL CELLS

The PEM is considered one of the most promising types of fuel cells for transportation. It can also be used to provide electricity for power plants, homes, and businesses.

The basic structure of a PEM fuel cell somewhat resembles a sandwich. Its layers are made up of two main parts: hardware and a membrane electrode assembly. The hardware of a PEM fuel cell makes up the outermost layer of a fuel cell, similar to the bread of a sandwich. The inside, the membrane electrode assembly, also contains several layers. Its outside layers consist of an anode on one side and a cathode on the other. The catalyst lies inside the anode/cathode layer. The innermost layer is a proton exchange membrane. The membrane is made up of a treated material that looks like plastic wrap. It contains the electrolyte.

A PEM fuel cell »

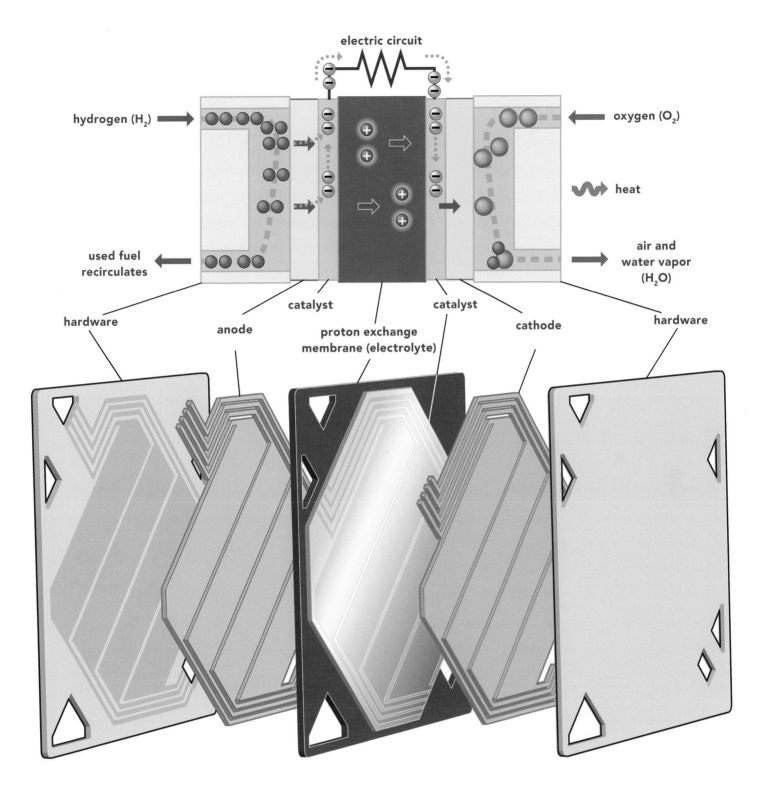

Pure hydrogen is fed through the anode via the hardware at one end. Air, which is rich in oxygen, is fed through the cathode via the hardware at the other end. A platinum catalyst speeds the chemical reaction, and the hydrogen atom is split into protons and electrons at the anode. The positively charged hydrogen protons flow through the membrane to the cathode. The electrons and heavier gases like oxygen cannot get across the membrane. The electrons instead flow into the electrical wiring to the cathode. Along the way they also provide electricity that can be connected to a grid and used to power everything from appliances to buildings. At the cathode the electrons, hydrogen protons, and oxygen from the air recombine to form water. The waste products from the PEM fuel cell are heat and water. The hardware layers, which are often made of carbon, conduct the flowing electrons and manage the water byproduct. This is important, because if the fuel cell has too much or too little water it can stop functioning.

PHOSPHORIC ACID FUEL CELLS

Another type of fuel cell that uses hydrogen as fuel is the PAFC. It uses phosphoric acid as an electrolyte and platinum as a catalyst. This type of cell has most commonly been used to provide power to buildings and power plants. Some have also been used to power transit buses. PAFCs tolerate impurities in the hydrogen fuel better than other fuel cells, but they are less powerful and more expensive than other fuel cells. They are also bigger and heavier than

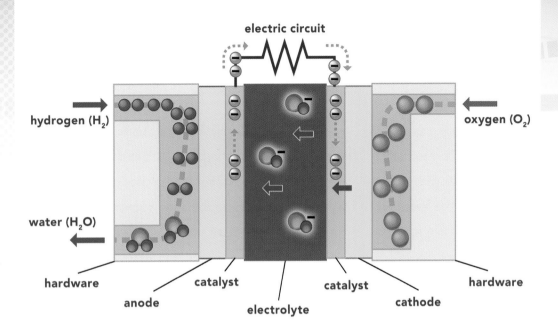

electric circuit

hydrogen (H_2)

water (H_2O)

oxygen (O_2)

hardware   anode   catalyst   electrolyte   catalyst   cathode   hardware

Alkali fuel cells work similar to PEM fuel cells and PAFCs, but water is expelled on the side where hydrogen enters.

other fuel cells. They also require a long warm-up period, but if engineers could overcome this limitation, PAFCs could someday be used more widely in vehicles.

ALKALINE FUEL CELLS

The AFC, pioneered by Bacon, is another design. AFCs have been the fuel cell of choice in the space program for decades, used to provide electric power and drinking water on board spacecraft. They operate on compressed hydrogen and oxygen and use a solution of potassium hydroxide in water as the electrolyte. The catalyst can be made of a variety of nonprecious metals. These fuel cells achieve high operating efficiencies and can be made of inexpensive materials. But they are prone to contamination by carbon dioxide and therefore require highly purified oxygen and hydrogen, which drives up the cost. They also have a limited lifespan. They can operate for 15,000 hours.[2] However, experts say they would need to operate for 40,000 hours or more to achieve commercial viability.[3] Although AFCs are not currently used in vehicles, they could be someday if engineers can find a way to purge carbon dioxide from their systems and extend their operating lives.

FUEL CELL USES

Fuel cells are made in many sizes and have many potential uses. Fuel cells offer many advantages when it comes to transportation. Today, several models of cars and buses powered by fuel cells, rather than a traditional internal combustion engine, are already on the road. Fuel cells are efficient and quiet and can be refueled in about the time it takes to refill a tank of gas.

Tiny PEM fuel cells could someday power cell phones, handheld computer games, and laptop computers. Larger PEM and PAFC fuel cells could be used to power homes, offices, and factories. Hydrogen-powered fuel cells have already been put to use for this purpose in hospitals and schools.

Some fuel cells, called solid polymer electrolysis units, can work in reverse. Like other fuel cells, they can make electricity, and, when run in reverse, they can also use electricity to make more hydrogen. These kinds of fuel cells could replace diesel generators to provide emergency backup power for buildings. When electricity is flowing, the fuel cells would use the electricity to make hydrogen. Then the hydrogen could be stored in large tanks. If the power goes out, the hydrogen could be used to power the building. Power companies could use these types of fuel cells to manage the demand for electricity, storing surplus energy as hydrogen gas. The stored hydrogen can be converted back into electricity at times when the demand for power is great.

Fuel cells have many advantages. They are reliable, efficient, and quiet. Their uses are diverse, from transportation to stationary power generation. Additionally, they have low emissions and can be a clean power source when their hydrogen is made from nonpolluting sources. But fuel cells can be heavy, costly, and have a

FUEL CELL STACKS

Single fuel cells do not provide much power: less than one volt, or enough to power a lightbulb.[4] Therefore, to create more power, several fuel cells are combined together in what are called fuel cell stacks. Depending on the power desired, stacks can consist of a small number of fuel cells to hundreds. Because its functions are synchronized, a fuel cell stack is often referred to simply as a fuel cell in scientific discussions.

"We're at the beginning of an exciting new era . . . to change the way we live—for the better. It is great to be one of the pioneers testing these cutting-edge fuel cells. We hope this fuel cell installation will lead to more widespread adoption of this technology, which could mean a cleaner future for everyone."[5]—**Alison Lewis, president of Coca-Cola-owned beverage company Odwalla, which installed fuel cells at its California packaging plant in 2010**

limited lifespan. Engineers are working to overcome these barriers for wider use. For instance, researchers at the Georgia Institute of Technology are looking at ways to make the membrane and catalysts in a PEM fuel cell more durable. Engineers at Apple are working to design lighter fuel cells. They imagine creating electronic devices with fuel cells built in. These devices, the Apple engineers say, could go weeks without recharging.

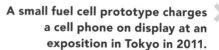

A small fuel cell prototype charges a cell phone on display at an exposition in Tokyo in 2011.

CHAPTER 7

HYDROGEN CARS

As the cost of gasoline climbs along with worries about carbon dioxide emissions, carmakers are investigating other fuels that can power cars. General Motors, Ford, Honda, BMW, and other carmakers all have programs to develop cars that run on hydrogen.

There are currently two different kinds of hydrogen cars on the road. One generates electricity from a fuel cell. The other uses an internal combustion engine (ICE) fueled by hydrogen.

FUEL CELL VEHICLES

A fuel cell vehicle is basically an electric car. But unlike electric cars, which store electricity in a battery, a fuel cell car produces its own electricity. PEM fuel cells are a primary focus in fuel cell vehicle research.

« **Several carmakers have created fuel cell vehicle models, such as this Mercedes-Benz B-class F-Cell.**

Within a fuel cell car, hydrogen is stored inside a tank and then fed into a fuel cell. The PEM fuel cell, which is about the size of a suitcase, acts like an onboard power plant. It makes electricity that powers the motor and in turn spins the wheels. In some fuel cell cars, such as the Honda Clarity, a battery can kick in when needed to supplement the car's power.

Although fuel cell cars work differently than conventional gasoline-powered cars, carmakers design them to look and feel like any other car. Drivers press pedals on the floor and turn a steering wheel to operate the vehicle, the same as in any other. But one thing sets these cars apart. "The difference is the silence while you drive," said Matthias Brock of Daimler's research and development department. "You hear almost nothing from the engine."[1]

Engineers overcame a number of challenges in developing these cars. As with most vehicles, they must work efficiently at all temperatures, including extreme cold. Experiments in Iceland, Norway, and Canada proved hydrogen cars can stand up to the test—they started at temperatures below minus 13 degrees Fahrenheit (−25°C).[2]

Finding a way to store enough hydrogen so that the car could travel long distances between fuel-ups was another challenge engineers faced. Compared by weight to gasoline, hydrogen has three times more energy, but when compared by volume, hydrogen gas has one-third of the energy of gasoline.[3] Storing a large enough volume of hydrogen gas to power a car for as long

Hydrogen gets fed into the fuel cell, which sits under the hood of a fuel cell vehicle, similar to a traditional engine.

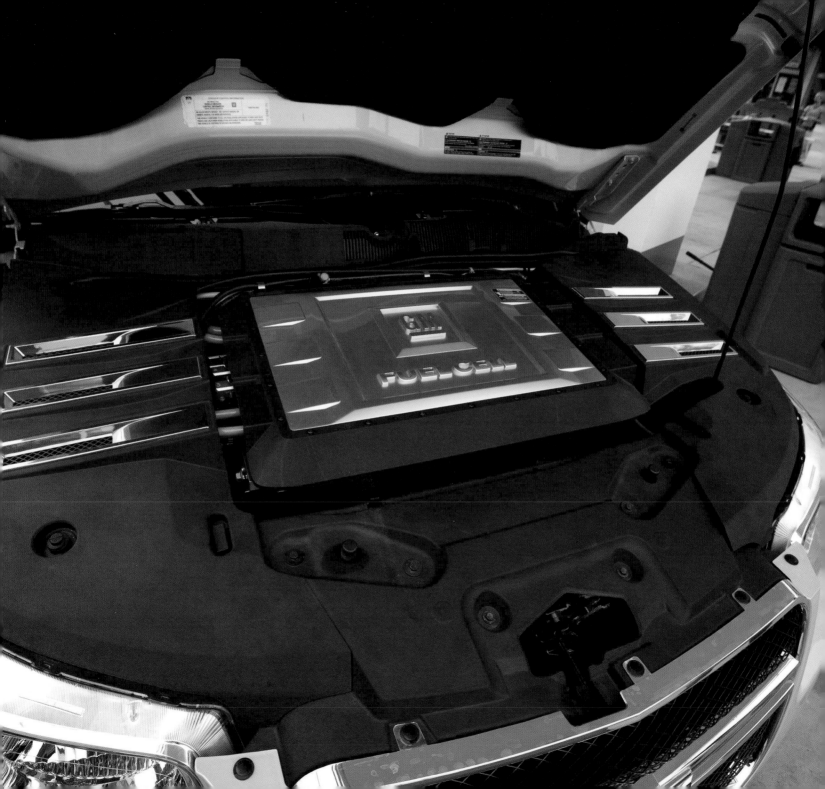

as a tank of gasoline would require huge storage tanks. The solution is storing hydrogen in high-pressure tanks, which makes it more compact and allows more of it to be stored onboard so that these cars can go longer distances. Daimler's latest fuel cell engines have a range of about 250 miles (400 km).[4] Researchers hope to achieve even better ranges in the future.

Cost was another obstacle—early versions of fuel cell cars cost approximately $1 million each to produce.[5] By 2011, the cost had only come down to approximately $100,000.[6] One factor driving up the cost was the small quantity being made. "When we have a dedicated assembly line and we calculate with scale in 2015 to 2020, what the price will be then is what's relevant," said Stephen Ellis, manager of fuel cell marketing for American Honda Motor Company.[7] Many carmakers claim mass production will bring the cost down further. Fuel cell vehicles may one day cost the same as other cars.

Fuel cell vehicles' biggest advantage is their potential to deliver big reductions in carbon emissions, as long as their hydrogen is produced in environmentally friendly ways. Disadvantages include the high cost of the fuel cells and the challenge of storing the large volumes of hydrogen needed to fuel the cars. Researchers continue making strides in bringing down cost and improving storage. However, one obstacle that still must be overcome for fuel cell vehicles to achieve widespread use is creating a nationwide refueling infrastructure.

« **A hydrogen tank is placed on a Honda Clarity during production in 2008. Hydrogen gas tanks are pressurized to store greater volume.**

FUEL CELL CAR COMPETITION: PLUG-IN HYBRID VEHICLES

Fuel cell vehicles also face heavy competition, mainly from plug-in hybrid electric vehicles (PHEVs). Just like a conventional hybrid, PHEVs are powered by both gasoline and electricity, and the electricity is stored in a battery. But in a PHEV, the battery can be recharged by plugging the car into an electric outlet.

Fuel cell cars have advantages and disadvantages when compared with PHEVs or electric cars powered by a battery. "The battery-powered cars are good for short trips and city driving," said Brock. "The fuel cell electric cars are better for longer ranges and have shorter refueling times."[8]

One disadvantage for fuel cell cars is the lack of fueling stations, whereas PHEVs can refuel via their second source

"A simple chemical reaction between hydrogen and oxygen generates energy, which can be used to power a car producing only water, not exhaust fumes. With a new national commitment, our scientists and engineers will overcome obstacles to taking these cars from laboratory to showroom so that the first car driven by a child born today could be powered by hydrogen, and pollution-free.[9]"

—**President George W. Bush, State of the Union address, January 28, 2003**

of power, gasoline, at any standard gas station. Yet charging the other half of the PHEV's power source, the battery, takes several hours, which is a distinct disadvantage. The fueling time for a fuel cell car is only a few minutes.

A 2009 study conducted by C. E. Thomas of H_2Gen Innovations, a Virginia company that makes reformers that convert natural gas into hydrogen, found that fuel cell vehicles would reduce carbon dioxide emissions more than PHEVs.[10] This is due to PHEVs' partial dependence on electricity. Most electricity in the United States is made by burning coal, which creates a lot of carbon dioxide emissions. It is important to also consider how the hydrogen for fuel cell vehicles was made, however, as some hydrogen production processes, such as electrolysis, use electricity as well.

Another reason evaluating hydrogen production for fuel cell vehicles is important is because today, most hydrogen is made from natural gas. This process creates more carbon dioxide

CROSS-COUNTRY CRUISE

On March 4, 2012, Cliff Ricketts, a professor at Middle Tennessee State University's School of Agribusiness and Agriscience, set out to drive across the country. No common road trip, Ricketts's goal was to use less than 10 gallons of gasoline on a 2,582-mile (4,155 km) journey. Ricketts and his team would divide the drive between three vehicles: a Toyota Tercel, an ICE vehicle, and a Toyota Prius, an electric-internal combustion engine hybrid, transformed to run on solar power and hydrogen from water for the first parts of the trip, and another Toyota Prius powered by battery power and ethanol to make the last leg of the drive. Ricketts stated that the first 900 miles (1,448 km) of the trip, from Savannah, Georgia, to Conway, Arkansas, the vehicles ran off sun and hydrogen from water. The trip, expected to take 5 days, took an hour less than Ricketts and his team anticipated. And the gasoline used? Only 2.15 gallons—more than 7 gallons less than their goal—was used in the trip. Ricketts said, "I feel like I climbed Mount Everest. This has significance in life and it has significance for mankind."[11]

than burning gasoline does. In that case, switching from gasoline to hydrogen does not make a lot of sense. But if hydrogen is made using renewable energy—solar, wind, or biomass—then replacing gasoline with hydrogen could help bring down carbon dioxide emissions.

In May 2007, two advanced hydrogen-powered fuel cell cars drove 300 miles (483 km) across the state of New York. "It was the world's first 300-mile drive that was petroleum-free and emissions-free on a single tank of fuel," said Larry Burns, head of research and development for General Motors, which designed the vehicles.[12]

For now, commercialization of hydrogen cars lags behind those of PHEVs. A few PHEVs are currently on the market, while hydrogen cars might not be available for purchase until 2015.[13] In the long run, either technology could prevail, which is why most major car companies are developing a mix of alternative vehicles.

INTERNAL COMBUSTION ENGINE HYDROGEN CARS

Another option being researched is using hydrogen to power a car that has a traditional ICE. Hydrogen ICE cars can be made to run on various types of fuel, such as hydrogen, ethanol, and gasoline. Some hydrogen ICE cars are on the road today, such as BMW's H-7, which can run on hydrogen or gasoline, switching between fuels with the push of a button. The H-7 has two

Mazda's Premacy Hydrogen RE Hybrid is an ICE hybrid vehicle that runs on gasoline and hydrogen and became available for commercial leasing in 2009.

separate fuel tanks, one for gasoline and one for hydrogen. The hydrogen is stored in a double-walled, stainless-steel vacuum tank that keeps it cold enough to stay liquid.

When running in hydrogen mode, the H-7 gives off almost no carbon dioxide. The only emissions are water vapor and tiny amounts of other gases.

One test driver noticed little difference in the H-7 when the car was running on hydrogen as opposed to gasoline mode. "Punch the throttle in either mode and the car rockets right away," he said.[14]

Hydrogen ICE cars offer advantages over gasoline-powered cars: reduced pollution, reduced dependence on foreign oil, and greater efficiency. The efficiency comes from being able to use a compression-ignition engine, which creates its own spark to light the fuel, with hydrogen. A spark-ignition engine, the type used for gasoline, requires a spark to be applied in order to create combustion.

Although hydrogen ICE vehicles have advantages, many experts believe the future of hydrogen cars lies mainly in fuel cell technology. But the need for a refueling infrastructure is a major roadblock to both fuel cell and hydrogen ICE cars. Some carmakers continue to research and develop hydrogen ICE cars as a faster step toward creating a hydrogen-powered economy.

As S. David Freeman, chair of the California Consumer Power and Conservation Financing Authority, puts it, "If we start to make hydrogen-burning cars immediately, we will bring on the infrastructure that will make it possible for fuel cell cars to come sooner."[15] By creating a demand for hydrogen, many carmakers are hoping these cars will help move the hydrogen economy forward.

"We're prepared to make thousands of these cars. But it really comes down to how many fuel stations there are at that point."[16]—**Mike O'Brien, vice president of product planning at Hyundai Motor America, on fuel cell vehicles**

On a sunny afternoon, magazine editor John Tayman steers a car through the hills north of San Francisco, California. He speeds past towering redwoods and weaves through ribbons of fog. Glancing at the fuel gauge, he realizes he is running low on hydrogen. He need only punch a button on the steering wheel labeled "H_2" and the car's engine will switch seamlessly to gasoline mode.

According to executives at BMW, this car may be a preview of what driving will be like in the future. Tayman is driving BMW's Hydrogen 7 (H-7). The car can do 143 mph and looks similar to an ordinary car. The interior also looks almost like the inside of any other luxury car. The most notable differences are the H_2 button on the steering wheel and a fire extinguisher beneath the front passenger seat.

Unlike a conventional car, the H-7 has two fuel tanks, one for gasoline and one for hydrogen. The car can travel 310 miles (499 km) on gas and another 125 miles (201 km) on hydrogen.[17] To keep the hydrogen liquefied for easy storage, the tank is cooled to several hundred degrees below zero. The tank is made of double-walled stainless steel. BMW has thoroughly tested the double-walled tanks: they have been cooked over high heat, violently shaken, and rammed with a giant pole to simulate the impact of a crash. After sitting in a fire for 10 minutes, safety valves began to leak hydrogen. The escaping gas caught fire but did not harm the tank.[18]

A BMW H-7 navigates the road seamlessly alongside traditional vehicles.

The double-walled tank acts like a super-charged thermos, providing the insulating power of 56 feet (17 m) of Styrofoam. If you poured in a scalding cup of hot chocolate in April, your drink would still be steaming at your Fourth of July picnic.[19] The water vapor that puffs out of the tail pipe of the H-7 when in hydrogen mode is so clean you can collect it in a glass and drink it.

BMW has spent millions of dollars developing the H-7. Other major car companies, such as Honda, General Motors, and Ford, have also spent millions developing their own hydrogen cars. Advocates of hydrogen say cars that use both gasoline and hydrogen, such as the H-7, can serve as transitional vehicles until the world builds a hydrogen infrastructure. BMW is working on a hydrogen-only car for when that day comes, if it arrives at all. As Tayman puts it, "The noble goal of the H-7 is, at heart, to save the earth."[20]

CHAPTER 8

THE FUTURE OF HYDROGEN

How big of a role will hydrogen have in the future? It could be a decade or two before anyone knows. Some think hydrogen will be central, the way petroleum has been for the past 100 years. Others think hydrogen will be used alongside other fuels.

HYDROGEN ECONOMY

Imagine living in a world powered by hydrogen. In this world, homes, hospitals, and schools make their own electricity from tanks of hydrogen. Nonpolluting cars, trucks, and buses powered by hydrogen dominate the roads. Hydrogen refueling stations dot the highways. This vision is often called the hydrogen economy, a system imagined by many scientists, politicians, and visionaries, in which a large portion of goods and

« **Many visualize a hydrogen economy in which hydrogen is easy to access and readily available to power cars, homes, and businesses.**

services are powered by hydrogen. It is a vision for a world fundamentally different than the one we live in today, and reaching it would take extraordinary measures.

The United States produces enough hydrogen to power 34 million cars, but most hydrogen produced is used in industry.[1] Converting to a hydrogen economy adapted for transportation would be a big job. The United States is currently set up as an oil economy. A lot of construction would be needed to develop a hydrogen infrastructure. Today there are 220,000 miles (354,000 km) of oil pipelines in the United States, versus less than 700 miles (1,130 km) of hydrogen pipelines. And there are 175,000 gasoline fueling stations in the country, versus fewer than 100 for hydrogen.[2] Most of the hydrogen stations were built to support demonstration projects, such as hydrogen-powered buses.

Developing a hydrogen economy would also require big changes in how fuel is produced, delivered, and used. It would also require

THE HYDROGEN HOUSE

Imagine living in a house that made its own energy from sunlight and water. A house like this exists in New Jersey. It looks like any other house, but it is powered by hydrogen. Fifty-six solar panels on the garage roof turn sunlight into electricity. Inside the house, an electrolyzer about the size of a washing machine uses the electricity to produce hydrogen. The hydrogen is then stored inside tanks, and a fuel cell is used to produce electricity from the stored hydrogen. The homeowner also has a hydrogen-powered car and lawn mower.

advances in devices that are powered by hydrogen, such as fuel cells. In other words, the hydrogen economy will not appear overnight.

INVESTMENT IN RESEARCH

Governments and corporations all over the world are investing millions of dollars in testing the possibilities of a hydrogen economy. One challenge to reaching a hydrogen economy is cost. Hydrogen would need to be similar in cost to other fuels. The price of the devices that use hydrogen would also need to be lower. Right now fuel cells are expensive. They would need to be lower in price to compete with traditional power systems.

The same goes for hydrogen cars. Fuel cell cars currently cost approximately $100,000.[3] That price is too expensive for the average driver. To convert an ICE vehicle to a hydrogen ICE costs approximately $5,000.[4] Fuel cell cars and hydrogen ICE cars both need to store enough hydrogen so they can drive long distances on a single tank of fuel, just as conventional cars do.

Car and energy companies have teamed with governments to support hydrogen projects. For instance, car company Daimler and energy companies Royal Dutch Shell and Norsk Hydro helped launch a hydrogen bus project that integrated dozens of fuel cell–powered buses into bus routes in ten cities in Europe and elsewhere. The project was funded by the European Union.

But some say it will take much more for hydrogen cars to become successful. As writer Joseph J. Romm describes getting the hydrogen economy started: "Who will spend hundreds of billions of dollars on a wholly new nationwide infrastructure . . . until millions of hydrogen vehicles are on the road? Yet who will manufacture and market such vehicles—and who will buy them—until the infrastructure is in place to fuel those vehicles?"[5]

HYDROGEN HIGHWAYS

Hydrogen highways are a key feature of a hydrogen economy. These are roads with a number of well-spaced hydrogen fueling stations, so that a fuel cell car would be able to travel the highway without running out of fuel.

Hydrogen highways are in the works around the world. In Norway, a hydrogen highway is being built with five or six hydrogen filling stations. The hydrogen will be produced from wind and solar energy. Hydrogen highways are being developed in British Columbia, Canada, and California. Both highways launched in 2004. The pilot program in Canada ended in 2011 and resulted in five hydrogen fueling stations. In California in 2004, it was announced that as many as 200 hydrogen stations were to be built along main Californian highways by 2010. However, only approximately 25 to 30 stations were built by 2011.

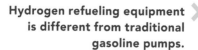

Hydrogen refueling equipment is different from traditional gasoline pumps.

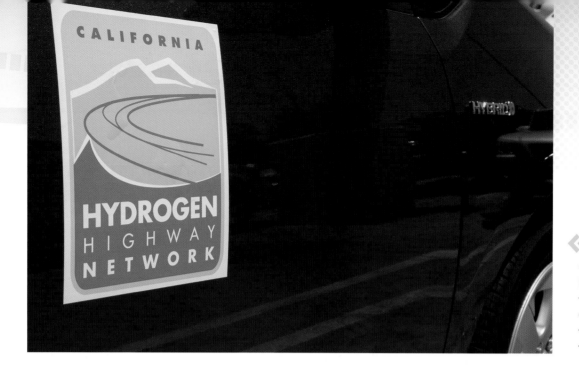

California opened its first hydrogen fueling station in 1992. California has more than 25 stations—more than any other state.

NATIONAL HYDROGEN LEADER

Although the highway fueling station program seemed to have stalled in California by 2011, the state has taken the lead in hydrogen economy development in the United States. In 1999, automakers, energy companies, and government agencies formed the California Fuel Cell Partnership. The goal was to develop and test fuel cell vehicles in California. Although the partnership promoted fuel cell vehicle use, energy companies were involved because the partnership's goals included finding ways to profit from new fuels, a concept these companies are invested in as well.

Hundreds of fuel cell vehicles now are on the road in California. These are mostly fuel cell buses and early, precommercial versions of hydrogen cars. Many car companies have handed out early-phase hydrogen cars to certain high-status individuals, such as celebrities, to pave the way for commercialization. More hydrogen vehicles are on the way. California also has dozens of fueling stations, more than any other part of the United States. So far California's stations have been used mostly for research and development, but that is expected to change as more hydrogen stations become available to the public.

California's fueling stations operate in different ways. Some stations make their own hydrogen. Others have it delivered by tanker trucks. One hydrogen station in Orange County, California, is supplied by an innovative new power station. The station is powered by biogas made from wastewater at a water treatment plant. The biogas is fed into a fuel cell to produce hydrogen, heat, and electricity. The hydrogen is sent to a fueling station, which receives enough hydrogen to fuel 25 to 50 fuel cell vehicles a day.[6] The electricity produced by the biogas is used to power the wastewater treatment plant.

INTERNATIONAL HYDROGEN LEADER

If any country is poised to have the first hydrogen economy, it could be Germany. German carmaker Daimler realized that its plans to start mass-producing fuel cell vehicles were stalled by

ICELAND'S HYDROGEN ECONOMY

In 1998, the small country of Iceland declared its goal to create the world's first working hydrogen economy in hopes of weaning itself off fossil fuels. The person leading the way was chemist Bragi Áronson. To create a hydrogen economy, Iceland would bank on its vast energy resources. The country sits on top of the Mid-Atlantic Ridge, the intersection of two of Earth's tectonic plates. The country has so many hot springs that almost all homes and buildings are heated with geothermal energy. The plan was to use this energy to create a hydrogen economy. Geothermal energy would be used to generate electricity, and the electricity would be used to make hydrogen by splitting water. The hydrogen would then be made available at fueling stations. But by 2008, the only signs of progress were one filling station, a handful of hydrogen cars, and one fuel cell-powered whale-watching boat. What happened? The global financial crisis from 2007 to 2012 caused Iceland's largest banks to collapse, putting Iceland's hydrogen dreams on hold.

a lack of hydrogen filling stations. Although Germany currently has 30 hydrogen filling stations, only seven are available to the public.[7] Daimler decided to do something about it. Daimler and the Linde technology group have teamed up to become a driving force for the possible new economy.

Daimler and Linde are working to build 20 new hydrogen stations by 2015. The new stations will be located along main traffic routes between major cities including Berlin, Hamburg, Stuttgart, and Munich. It will then be possible for a hydrogen-powered vehicle to travel from city to city without running out of fuel. Daimler has indicated its willingness to partner with others in the fuel, energy, and automotive industries.

From front, hydrogen tanks, biofuel tanks, and a wind turbine in Germany at the world's first power station using renewable energy to create hydrogen

The project builds on some government programs that seek to increase the number of hydrogen filling stations and make hydrogen work for everyday uses, but it is not otherwise funded by the government. "It's not clear yet if the government will support this," said Matthias Brock of Daimler's research and development department. "But we'll build the hydrogen refueling network anyway."[8]

So will the world someday be powered by hydrogen? As the demand for power increases, and the need to find clean sources of energy rises, research and development will continue on many alternative energy sources. How big a role hydrogen will play in the future remains unclear. But innovations in production, creation, storage, and transport that are underway and on the horizon make harnessing hydrogen a viable future fuel option.

Innovations such as this hydrogen-powered motorbike in France have been developed in hopes of making hydrogen a part of the world's energy future.

GLOSSARY

ALKALINE—Chemically basic (having a pH value of greater than 7.0), such as sodium hydroxide or potassium hydroxide.

ARTIFICIAL LEAVES—Devices that convert solar energy to chemical fuel by coupling a solar collector that converts the sun's energy into electricity with an electrolyzer that splits water into oxygen and hydrogen.

BIOREACTORS—Vessels in which living organisms either produce substances or break down substances to create new ones.

CATALYST—A substance that aids a chemical reaction.

ELECTRODE—A terminal that conducts electric current in a device such as a battery, fuel cell, or electrolyzer.

ELECTROLYSIS—The process of passing an electric current through electrolytes to create chemical change.

ELECTROLYTE—A substance that, when in a liquid form or dissolved in a solvent, is capable of conducting an electric current.

ELECTROLYZER—An apparatus for carrying out electrolysis. It runs electricity through water, splitting it into hydrogen and oxygen.

ENERGY CARRIER—A substance, such as fuel, or a phenomenon, such as electricity, that can be used to do useful work.

GREENHOUSE GAS—A gas, such as carbon dioxide or methane, that contributes to global warming.

INFRASTRUCTURE—The basic facilities that allow a community, city, state, or country to operate, including roads, bridges, schools, and power plants.

INTERMITTENT—Something that starts and stops or only occurs irregularly.

MICROORGANISMS—Tiny organisms such as algae or bacteria.

PLATINUM—A precious metal that can be used as a catalyst for electrolysis.

UTILITY—An organization that supplies resources such as electricity, gas, and water for the public in a given area.

UTILITY GRID—System that generates, transmits, and distributes electricity over a vast area.

VOLTAGE—The electric potential or difference in electric charge between two points in an electric circuit.

ADDITIONAL RESOURCES

SELECTED BIBLIOGRAPHY

Hoffmann, Peter. *Tomorrow's Energy: Hydrogen, Fuel Cells, and the Prospects for a Cleaner Planet.* Cambridge, MA: MIT, 2001. Print.

Quaschning, Volker. *Renewable Energy and Climate Change.* West Sussex, UK: Wiley, 2010. Print.

Regalado, Antonio. "Reinventing the Leaf." *Scientific American.* Scientific American/Nature America, 2010. Web. 4 Oct 2012.

Romm, Joseph J. *The Hype About Hydrogen.* Washington, DC: Island, 2004. Print.

FURTHER READINGS

Backus, Albert O., ed. *Hydrogen Energy: Background, Significance And Future.* Hauppauge, NY: Novinka-Nova. 2006. Print.

Thaddeus, Eva. *Powering the Future: New Energy Technologies.* Albuquerque, NM: U of New Mexico P, 2010. Print.

WEB LINKS

To learn more about hydrogen and fuel cells, visit ABDO Publishing Company online at **www.abdopublishing.com**. Web sites about hydrogen and fuel cells are featured on our Book Links page. These links are routinely monitored and updated to provide the most current information available.

FOR MORE INFORMATION

For more information on this subject, contact or visit the following organizations:

US DEPARTMENT OF ENERGY: ENERGY EFFICIENCY & RENEWABLE ENERGY
Fuel Cell Technologies Program
1000 Independence Avenue SW, Washington DC 20585
202-586-5000
www1.eere.energy.gov/hydrogenandfuelcells

The EERE conducts research and development of hydrogen and fuel cell production. Contact the organization for more information on programs, manufacturing, safety standards, storage, and transportation of hydrogen and advances in fuel cell technology.

US DEPARTMENT OF ENERGY NATIONAL RENEWABLE ENERGY LABORATORY
15013 Denver West Parkway, Golden, CO 80401-3305
303-275-3000
www.nrel.gov

The National Renewable Energy Laboratory researches and develops innovations in renewable energy technology, including hydrogen and fuel cells.

SOURCE NOTES

CHAPTER 1. WHY HYDROGEN?

1. "H2 Educate: Student Guide." *US Department of Energy: Energy Efficiency and Renewable Energy.* US Department of Energy, 2005. Web. 4 Oct. 2012.

2. "Annual Energy Review." *US Energy Information Administration: Total Energy.* US Department of Energy, 27 Sept. 2012. Web. 4 Oct. 2012.

3. "Future Direction of the Department of Energy's Office of Science." *US House of Representatives Committee Hearings: Committee on Science.* US House of Representatives, 25 July 2002. Web. 4 Oct. 2012.

4. "Hydrogen & Our Energy Future." *US Department of Energy: Energy Efficiency and Renewable Energy.* US Department of Energy, n.d. Web. 4 Oct. 2012.

5. Ibid.

6. "The Current and Future Consequences of Climate Change." *NASA: Global Climate Change.* NASA, n.d. Web. 4 Oct. 2012.

7. Volker Quaschning. *Renewable Energy and Climate Change.* West Sussex, UK: Wiley, 2010. Print. 266.

CHAPTER 2. THE HISTORY OF HYDROGEN

1. Peter Hoffmann. *Tomorrow's Energy: Hydrogen, Fuel Cells, and the Prospects for a Cleaner Planet.* Cambridge, MA: MIT, 2001. Print. 234–235.

2. David Brown. "Hydrogen Didn't Cause Hindenburg Fire, UCLA Engineer, Former NASA Researcher Find." *UCLA News.* UCLA Engineering, 28 May 1998. Web. 4 Oct. 2012.

3. Volker Quaschning. *Renewable Energy and Climate Change.* West Sussex, UK: Wiley, 2010. Print. 266.

4. "Alkali Fuel Cells." *Fuel Cells.* Smithsonian Institution, 2009. Web. 4 Oct. 2012.

5. Bill Bowman. "1966 GM Electrovan." *GM Heritage Center.* General Motors, n.d. Web. 4 Oct. 2012.

6. Ibid.

7. Ibid.

CHAPTER 3. HYDROGEN PRODUCTION AND USES

1. "The Impact of Increased Use of Hydrogen on Petroleum Consumption and Carbon Dioxide Emissions." *US Energy Information Administration.* US Department of Energy, Aug. 2008. Web. 4 Oct. 2012.

2. "Hydrogen and Fuel Cells at NASA." *NASA.* NASA, 25 July 2012. Web. 4 Oct. 2012.

3. "Hydrogen & Our Energy Future." *US Department of Energy: Energy Efficiency and Renewable Energy.* US Department of Energy, n.d. Web. 4 Oct. 2012.

4. "Biomass Basics." *Energy Kids: US Energy Information Administration.* US Department of Energy, n.d. Web. 4 Oct. 2012.

5. "New Horizons for Hydrogen." *National Renewable Energy Laboratory.* US Department of Energy, Feb. 2011. Web. 4 Oct. 2012.

6. Thomas A. Milne, Carolyn C. Elam, and Robert J. Evans. "Hydrogen from Biomass: State of the Art and Research Challenge." *Hydrogen Implementing Agreement.* International Energy Agency, n.d. Web. 4 Oct. 2012.

7. Jessica Ebert. "Solar-Powered Biomass Gasification." *Biomass Magazine.* BBI International, n.d. Web. 4 Oct. 2012.

8. Antonio Regalado. "Reinventing the Leaf." *Scientific American*. Scientific American/Nature America, 2010. Web. 4 Oct. 2012.

9. "New Nuclear Energy Facilities Will Support Growth, Provide Clean Electricity." *Nuclear Energy Institute: Resources and Stats*. Nuclear Energy Institute, Apr. 2012. Web. 4 Oct. 2012.

10. "Benefits of Nuclear Energy." *Idaho National Laboratory*. US Department of Energy, n.d. Web. 4 Oct. 2012.

11. David Pacchioli. "Energy Unbound." *Penn State: Hydrogen*. Penn State University, 8 June 2005. Web. 4 Oct. 2012.

CHAPTER 4. NEW HORIZONS IN HYDROGEN PRODUCTION

1. Antonio Regalado. "Reinventing the Leaf." *Scientific American*. Scientific American/Nature America, 2010. Web. 4 Oct. 2012.

2. Ibid.

3. Ibid.

4. Ibid.

5. Lori Zimmer. "MIT Scientists Create Artificial Solar Leaf That Can Power Homes." *Inhabit*. Inhabit.com, 28 Mar. 2011. Web. 4 Oct. 2012.

6. Mark Brown. "MIT's Artificial Leaf is Ten Times More Efficient Than the Real Thing." *Wired.co.uk*. Condé Nast Digital, 28 Mar. 2011. Web. 4 Oct. 2012.

7. David Pacchioli. "Energy Unbound." *Penn State: Hydrogen*. Pennsylvania State University, 8 June 2005. Web. 4 Oct. 2012.

8. Ibid.

CHAPTER 5. HYDROGEN STORAGE AND TRANSPORT

1. Scott L. Montgomery. *The Powers That Be: Global Energy for the Twenty-First Century and Beyond*. Chicago: U of Chicago P, 2010. Print. 186.

2. David Pacchioli. "What Form Fits?" *Penn State: Hydrogen*. Pennsylvania State University, 8 June 2005. Web. 4 Oct. 2012.

3. Volker Quaschning. *Renewable Energy and Climate Change*. West Sussex, UK: Wiley, 2010. Print. 269.

4. "Hydrogen Basics." *Fuel Cells 2000*. FuelCells.org, 2012. Web. 4 Oct. 2012.

5. Bill Vincent. "Hydrogen and the Law: Safety and Liability." *Fuel Cells 2000*. FuelCells.org, 11 June 2004. Web. 4 Oct. 2012.

6. Louis Schlapbach. "Hydrogen-Fuelled Vehicles." *Nature* 13 Aug. 2009: 809–811. Print.

7. Michael R. Swain. "Fuel Leak Simulation." *US Department of Energy: Energy Efficiency & Renewable Program*. US Department of Energy, n.d. Web. 5 Oct. 2012.

CHAPTER 6. FUEL CELLS

1. David Pacchioli. "An Infinite Charge." *Penn State: Hydrogen*. Pennsylvania State University, 8 June 2005. Web. 5 Oct. 2012.

2. M. Cifrain and K. Kordesch. "Hydrogen/Oxygen (Air) Fuel Cells with Alkaline Electrolytes." *Handbook of Fuel Cells — Fundamentals, Technology and Applications, Volume I*. West Sussex, UK: Wiley, 2003. Print. 268.

3. "Types of Fuel Cells." *US Department of Energy: Energy Efficiency and Renewable Energy*. US Department of Energy, 19 Nov. 2010. Web. 5 Oct. 2012.

4. "Fuel Cell Technology." *USC: Center for Fuel Cells*. University of South Carolina, n.d. Web. 5 Oct. 2012.

5. *Fuel Cell and Hydrogen Energy Association*. Fuel Cell and Hydrogen Energy Association, n.d. Web. 28 Aug. 2012.

CHAPTER 7. HYDROGEN CARS

1. Climatewire. "Will Germany Become First Nation with a Hydrogen Economy?" *Scientific American*. Scientific American/Nature America, 25 Aug. 2011. Web. 5 Oct. 2012.

2. Ibid.

3. "Benefits and Challenges." *FuelEconomy.gov*. US Department of Energy, 5 Oct. 2012. Web. 5 Oct. 2012.

4. "Hydrogen Cars: Fad or the Future?" *EV World*. EVWorld.com, 5 June 2009. Web. 5 Oct. 2012.

5. Ibid.

6. Climatewire. "Will Germany Become First Nation with a Hydrogen Economy?" *Scientific American*. Scientific American/Nature America, 25 Aug. 2011. Web. 5 Oct. 2012.

7. Janet Whitman. "High Hopes, and Hurdles, for Hydrogen Cars." *USA Today: Cars*. USA Today/Gannet, 19 June 2011. Web. 5 Oct. 2012.

8. Climatewire. "Will Germany Become First Nation with a Hydrogen Economy?" *Scientific American*. Scientific American/Nature America, 25 Aug. 2011. Web. 5 Oct. 2012.

9. "Text of President Bush's 2003 State of the Union Address." *Washington Post*. Washington Post, 28 Jan. 2003. Web. 5 Oct. 2012.

10. C. E. Thomas. "Fuel Cell and Battery Electric Vehicles Compared." *Alternative Vehicle Comparisons*. C. E. Thomas, n.d. Web. 8 Oct. 2012.

11. "Tenn. Professor Cruises Cross-Country on 2.15 Gallons of Gas." *USA Today: News*. USA Today/Gannet, 9 Mar. 2012. Web. 5 Oct. 2012.

12. "Hydrogen Cars: Fad or the Future?" *EV World*. EVWorld.com, 5 June 2009. Web. 5 Oct. 2012.

13. "The Road Ahead." *Consumer Reports*. Consumer Reports, May 2010. Web. 20 Aug. 2012.

14. "Renewable Hydrogen Bus Teaches Thousands about Clean Energy Technologies." *National Renewable Energy Laboratory*. US Department of Energy, 6 June 2011. Web. 8 Oct. 2012.

15. Joseph J. Romm. *The Hype About Hydrogen*. Washington, DC: Island, 2004. Print. 116.

16. Janet Whitman. "High Hopes, and Hurdles, for Hydrogen Cars." *USA Today: Cars*. USA Today/Gannet, 19 June 2011. Web. 5 Oct. 2012.

17. John Tayman. "Steering for Tomorrow." *CNNMoney*. Cable News Network/Time Warner, 3 Apr. 2007. Web. 8 Oct. 2012.

18. Peter Hoffmann. *Tomorrow's Energy: Hydrogen, Fuel Cells, and the Prospects for a Cleaner Planet*. Cambridge, MA: MIT, 2001. Print. 128.

19. John Tayman. "Steering for Tomorrow." *CNNMoney*. Cable News Network/Time Warner, 3 Apr. 2007. Web. 8 Oct. 2012.

20. Ibid.

CHAPTER 8. THE FUTURE OF HYDROGEN

1. Michael Fitzgerald. "Hotbed." *Fast Company*. Mansueto Ventures, 1 Apr. 2008. Web. 8 Oct. 2012.

2. National Research Council and National Academy of Engineering. *The Hydrogen Economy: Opportunities, Costs, Barriers, and R&D Needs*. Washington, DC: National Academies, 2004. Print. 194.

3. Climatewire. "Will Germany Become First Nation with a Hydrogen Economy?" *Scientific American*. Scientific American/Nature America, 25 Aug. 2011. Web. 5 Oct. 2012.

4. Adam Campisi, et al. "Hydrogen Powered Vehicles." *Worcester Polytechnic Institute*. Worcester Polytechnic Institute, n.d. Web. 8 Oct. 2012.

5. Joseph J. Romm. *The Hype About Hydrogen*. Washington, DC: Island, 2004. Print. 20.

6. "Energy Department Applauds World's First Fuel Cell and Hydrogen Energy Station in Orange County." *Energy. gov*. US Department of Energy, 16 Aug. 2011. Web. 8 Oct. 2012.

7. Climatewire. "Will Germany Become First Nation with a Hydrogen Economy?" *Scientific American*. Scientific American/Nature America, 25 Aug. 2011. Web. 5 Oct. 2012.

8. Ibid.

>> INDEX

ABOUT THE AUTHOR

Dr. Rebecca Hirsch is a scientist-turned-writer and the author of many science books for young readers. She lives with her family in Pennsylvania.

ABOUT THE CONTENT CONSULTANT

Dr. Cliff Ricketts is a professor of agricultural education at the School of Agribusiness and Agriscience at Middle Tennessee State University. His areas of study include innovations in agricultural practices and transportation technology with a focus on alternative fuels including corn ethanol, soybean oil, and hydrogen from water. In 1992, Ricketts set a land speed record for a hydrogen vehicle that stood for 15 years. In 2012, he refitted three vehicles to make a cross-country drive powered largely by solar, hydrogen, and battery power. Ricketts is an active alternative fuel advocate and has spoken before the US Congress Committee on Science and Energy in support of clean fuel research and advancement.